"I was compelled to read Gleb Tsipursky's book, yet found myself fighting with his premise. What do you mean, don't go with my gut? Then I kept reading and applied his eight-step model to some major choices in front of me. Next, I reflected on a few disasters that perhaps could have been avoided if I had this book earlier. With practical tips and takeaways, and research to support the methodology, this book will be on my recommendation list for the leaders whom I coach and train and added to my personal favorites."—Barb Girson, CEO and founder of My Sales Tactics, LLC

"It's the oldest problem in the world. It's even mentioned in the Book of Genesis. How do you keep the tools the Good Lord gave us from getting in our own way? Gleb has written a really interesting book here about how we might go about solving that."—Hugh MacLeod, lead artist and cofounder, Gapingvoid LLC; bestselling author, *Ignore Everybody*

"You can't make a better decision than to read this gem of a book that provides you with a practical framework for making the right and effective decisions."—Bala V. Sathyanarayanan, senior vice president and chief human resources officer, Greif Inc.

"*Never Go With Your Gut* is an entertaining and highly practical guide to avoiding the pitfalls and biases that trip up even the most experienced leaders."—Todd Henry, bestselling author, *Die Empty* and *The Accidental Creative*

"I highly recommended it for all decision-makers, leaders, and those looking to become leaders."—Carolina Thatcher, MPA, diversity and inclusion expert

"Trust is your most valuable asset. Why leave it to the insatiability and impulsivity of your gut?"—Kurt Roemer, chief security strategist, Citrix Systems

"For anyone who values themselves, their time, the work they offer to the world, and all the people whose lives they touch, I highly recommend reading, absorbing, and applying the truth in this book."—Pat Lynch, CEO of Women's Radio

"This book provides a very insightful set of lenses to understand the errors and biases that creep into our decision-making in such situations."—Jay Anand, PhD, academic director of the Ohio State Center for Innovation and Entrepreneurship

"As an expert in how to truly build wealth and escape mainstream myths through the power of entrepreneurship, I can attest that this groundbreaking book is badly needed! If you want to succeed in the world of tomorrow, pick up a copy of this book today."—MJ Demarco, CEO of Viperion Publishing Corp.; bestselling author, *The Millionaire Fastlane* and *Unscripted*

"As an experienced healthcare CEO, I have seen too many leaders make poor decisions by following their gut reactions. If you want to protect yourself and others in your organization from dangerous judgment errors, make sure to get this groundbreaking book!"—Randy Oostra, PhD, president and CEO, ProMedica Health System

"Before you find yourself about to make another gut-based decision that will surely end badly you must take the time to read this book. It will save you from yourself!"—Leonard A. Schlesinger, PhD, vice chairman and COO Emeritus, Limited Brands, Baker Foundation; professor, Harvard Business School; and bestselling author, *Just Start*

"In a world here human knowledge is doubling every twelve hours, the temptation for seasoned leaders to sacrifice research for expedience and 'go with their gut' has never been greater and never been more at risk for failure. Gleb Tsipursky provides insightful descriptions of the source of these biases and outlines proven strategies and tactics for applying data-driven techniques to significantly improve the quality of our decisions."—Steven Johnson, LLD, president and CEO, University of Pittsburgh Medical Center Susquehanna

"Business leaders can and should implement these practices so as to avoid the costly mistakes that often lead to disastrous outcomes for their enterprises."
—Michael A. Roberto, PhD, bestselling author, *Unlocking Creativity* and *Know What You Don't Know;* and Trustee Professor of Management, Bryant University

"How often do we talk ourselves into a decision because it feels good or it feels right, only to have remorse soon (or at some point) thereafter? Gleb's book dives deep into the quagmire of cognitive biases that cloud our judgments and decisions, and then pulls us out and rescues us from those traps."—Kirk Borne, PhD, principal data scientist and executive advisor, Booz Allen Hamilton

"It doesn't matter if you have been a business owner for decades or just recently become one. This book is an absolute MUST purchase."—Michelle Jeralds, agency owner of Brightway Insurance, The Michelle Jeralds Agency

"Gleb Tsipursky has engineered simple-to-apply concepts for achieving your goals."—Michael LaRosa, CEO, LaRosa's Family Pizzerias

Praise for *Never Go With Your Gut*

"One of the biggest traps business leaders fall into is when they believe they are right when in fact they are very wrong. No one reading this engaging and practical book can walk away believing they are immune to bias; anyone reading this book will now be armed with practical techniques to stop making the same mistakes over and over again."—Sydney Finkelstein, PhD, professor of leadership at Dartmouth College; bestselling author, *Superbosses* and *Why Smart Executives Fail*; and host of *The Sydcast*

"Combining the author's practical business experience as a management consultant with cutting-edge research in behavioral economics and cognitive neuroscience, this book provides strategies and techniques that any business leader will find helpful."—Brian P. Moran, bestselling author, *The 12 Week Year*

"Becoming a great business leader—just like becoming a millionaire—doesn't take genius, but it does take making wise decisions and avoiding bad ones. This book shows that our decision-making can be easily improved. It helps leaders notice when their emotions are driving them to make poor decisions, and provides clear and easy strategies to improve judgment calls, for individuals, and teams alike."—William D. Danko, PhD, bestselling author, *The Millionaire Next Door* and *Richer than a Millionaire;* Professor Emeritus, School of Business, State University of New York at Albany

"Because life doesn't come with an undo button, all leaders should read *Never Go With Your Gut.*"—Judy Robinett, bestselling author, *How to be a Power Connector* and *Crack the Funding Code*

"This is a compelling and much needed book. Its sage advice could not be offered (or heeded) soon enough."—Amy C. Edmondson, PhD, professor at Harvard Business School; bestselling author, *The Fearless Organization* and *Teaming*

"The antidote for a hustle economy run by the seat of your pants, Dr. Tsipursky carves a rational path forward for business strategy based on data, insight, and proven best practices."—Mark Schaefer, bestselling author, *Marketing Rebellion* and *The Content Code;* professor, Rutgers University

GLEB TSIPURSKY, PHD CEO, Disaster Avoidance Experts

NEVER GO WITH YOUR GUT

How Pioneering Leaders
Make the Best Decisions and
Avoid Business Disasters

CAREER
PRESS

This edition first published in 2019 by Career Press, an imprint of
Red Wheel/Weiser, LLC
With offices at:
65 Parker Street, Suite 7
Newburyport, MA 01950
www.redwheelweiser.com
www.careerpress.com

ISBN: 978-1-63265-162-4
Library of Congress Cataloging-in-Publication Data available upon request.
Cover design by Kathryn Sky-Peck
Interior by Scriptorium Book Packagers
Typeset in Adobe Garamond Pro and Helvetica Neue

Printed in Canada
MAR
10 9 8 7 6 5 4 3 2 1

Dedication

This book is dedicated to all my clients: By honoring me with your trust and inviting me into your confidence, you enabled me to gain the experience and insights needed to write this book. Thank you from the bottom of my heart.

Contents

Acknowledgments

Going against the grain of traditional leadership advice can be a lonely journey. I am incredibly grateful to the many people who risked collaborating with me by departing from the mainstream and instead followed the counterintuitive revelations of cutting-edge research on avoiding dangerous judgment errors. Thanks to their support, I can do my small part to address the deep suffering caused by disastrous decisions that ruin highly profitable companies, top-notch careers, and great business relationships.

First, both now and always, I'm truly fortunate to have a life partner who is also my business partner. I truly can't imagine my life without you, Agnes Vishnevkin. Your support, professional and personal, was the most important factor that enabled me to write this book.

My thanks to the people who gave feedback on early versions of this book: Alex Fleiss, Artie Isaac, Jeff Dubin, Mark Faust, Michael Tyler, Susan Lear, and Wayne Straight (who also contributed his graphic skills). Howard Ross not only gave feedback but also generously contributed his wisdom and experience in the foreword. The moral and professional support of fellow speakers in the Ohio chapter of the National Speaker's Association helped uplift my writing.

My gratitude to my literary agent, Linda Konner, who saw the potential in my manuscript and worked hard to find a worthwhile publisher. I greatly appreciate all the folks at Career Press, especially my editor Michael Pye, a staunch advocate and supporter for this contrarian and iconoclastic work.

I would never have been able to write this book without my clients. They taught me so much about what happens when the rubber of cutting-edge research meets the road of everyday business reality.

Their stories represent the heart of this work, and for this, I bow to them with gratitude.

Finally, my thanks to you, the readers of this book. Without you reading it, my work has no meaning. I very much hope that your journey with this book will empower you to avoid the disasters that result from falling into dangerous judgment errors. I am eager to hear about your experience.

I take full responsibility for any mistakes: please bring them to my attention by emailing me at *Gleb@DisasterAvoidanceExperts.com*. You can share other forms of feedback and your experience with the book by emailing me and/or visiting the book's website, *www.DisasterAvoidanceExperts.com/NeverGut.com*, where you can submit your thoughts for a public post.

Foreword

Right from the front cove, this book challenges us. The very notion of *Never Go with Your Gut* seems anathema at a time when so many are telling us to do the exact opposite: "Trust your instincts," "Go with your intuition," and make decisions in a "blink," or rely on "what you feel." We are choosing leaders based on how they make us feel, rather than what they know and can do. Of course, understanding our emotional reactions is valuable, and there may, in fact, be times when our instincts are on point and where quick decisions work out, but as Gleb Tsipursky has shown us in this valuable text, that is often just plain dumb luck, and more often can lead to challenges, problems, or even disaster.

Gleb has done an excellent job of helping us understand why "gut instincts" are severely limited as a way to make important life decisions. He breaks down our all-too-human thinking in a way that helps us understand that the very instincts we use are actually designed for another time in human evolution. It's not that our automatic way of thinking is never valuable. As Daniel Kahneman has been known to say, when you are driving and the car in front of you stops short, and their tail lights come on, it's not the time to go to your "intentional" brain and contemplate what the best thing to do is in the situation. That is a recipe for ending up in the back seat of the car in front of you.

However, the challenge is that the most important of life's decisions are best made with more thoughtful consideration of the situation at hand, the options available, and the predictable outcomes of our decisions. All of us, of course, know this. We have all made the mistake of going with the quick decision, the one that "feels" right only to find that dating that person, taking that job, making that investment, or voting for that person was probably not such a great idea. And how many times have we looked back only to see clearly in hindsight all of the clues that were right in front of us, shouting out what a bad idea it was…yet we did it anyway.

The thing I like about Gleb's work, and particularly the way he approaches it in this book, is that he demonstrates his own work in the way he shares it with us. This is not a book written by an author who is just opining about his point of view. Gleb meticulously builds his case by thoughtfully sharing the psychology and cognitive neuroscience behind his premise. He helps us understand why we do what we do, how it impacts us, and how we can make better decisions in a way that has us not only moved to take action but also understand why it is so important that we do.

Gleb gives great insight, from a scientific perspective, as to what causes us to make bad decisions, how our instincts may steer us wrong, and how to think in ways that are likely to create better results. He describes a pathway to making better decisions through understandable models that we can put to use every day, and even gives us exercises that cause us to develop a better understanding of why we do what we do, and how to do it better.

Gleb Tsipursky has given us a handbook for good decision-making. He has written a fascinating book, drawn from a broad range of intellectual understanding and perspectives. More importantly, it is a practical book that will help any reader make better decisions, especially the important ones, and impact their lives, their relationships, and their businesses in a positive way, including financially.

In a world in which we see leaders making terrible decisions, based on all of the wrong motivations, Gleb gives us hope that we can find a way to think carefully, choose wisely, and thrive because of it.

I, for one, am glad he wrote it, and I hope that business leaders and politicians alike read it and take it to heart. It will make them better. It will make all of us better.

—Howard J. Ross
Author of *Our Search for Belonging,*
Everyday Bias, and *ReInventing Diversity*

Introduction

The biggest falsehood in business leadership and career advice may also be the most repeated: "Go with your gut." Surely you hear this advice often, as well as some variations, such as, "Trust your instincts," "Be authentic," "Listen to your heart," or "Follow your intuition."

I'm deeply frustrated, saddened, and angered when I see highly profitable companies, top-notch careers, and great business relationships devastated because someone bought into the toxic advice of going with their gut. Someone returning home from a guru's seminar and starting to behave like their "authentic self" shoots themselves—and their business—in the foot. Our authentic selves are adapted for the ancient savanna, not the modern business world. Following your intuition in today's professional environment can lead to terrible decisions. For the sake of our bottom lines, we need to avoid following our primitive instincts, and instead, be civilized about how we address the inherently flawed nature of our minds.

In your company, what percent of projects suffer from cost overruns? When was the last time a leader resisted necessary changes? How often are people on your team overconfident about the quality of their decisions? What proportion of workplace plans overemphasize smaller short-term gains over larger long-term ones? How frequently are people reluctant to discuss potentially serious issues? All of these problems, and many others, come from following our gut reactions. You can see a longer list of issues and evaluate their impact on your workplace in the assessment in Chapter 7.

If repeated frequently enough, these mistakes can and do result in disasters for successful companies and bring down high-flying careers, especially when they face smart competitors who educate themselves on and avoid such problems. By contrast, if you are the one to learn about and defend yourself from these errors, you can take advantage of rivals who go with their guts and make devastating mistakes, which enables you to gain a serious competitive edge.

Tragically, current business strategic assessments meant to address the weaknesses of human nature through structures and planning are deeply flawed. The most popular of them, SWOT, has a group of business leaders figure out the strengths, weaknesses, opportunities, and threats facing their businesses. However, SWOT assessments usually fail to account for the dangerous judgment errors we make due to how our brain is wired—mistakes that are often exponentially increased in group settings. SWOT and similar strategic assessments give a false sense of comfort and security to business leaders who use them; these comforting techniques result in appalling oversights that ruin profitable businesses.

Surprisingly, sports have pulled ahead of the vast majority of business in recognizing the value of avoiding gut reactions, as popularized by the 2011 film *Moneyball*. The movie chronicles the 2002 season of the Oakland Athletics baseball team, which had a very limited budget for players that year. The general manager, Billy Beane, adopted a very unorthodox approach of relying on quantitative data and statistics to choose players: He used his head rather than the traditional method of trusting the team scouts' intuitions and gut reactions. By hiring players who were undervalued by other teams that used old-school evaluation methods, the Oakland Athletics won a record-breaking twenty games in a row. Other teams have since adopted the same approach, and statistics now dominate over gut reactions in decision-making regarding players as well as what plays to make. Reliance on quantitative data has grown in popularity for other sports as well. For example, punting in football is decreasing because of evidence-based approaches that show punting is a bad idea statistically, despite gut reactions that suggest punting works well.

What if you could introduce a similar revolutionary innovation in your business that rewards you with record-breaking growth twenty quarters in a row? You will hit a home run when you go with your head and avoid your gut.

If our intuitions are such a bad match for the modern world, why is the advice to "go with your gut" so widespread? Because trusting our instincts feels comfortable. We tend to choose what's comfortable rather than what's true or good for us, even in the face of very strong evidence suggesting otherwise.

"Go with your gut" is the business advice equivalent of the chocolate caramel brownie with mint chocolate chip ice cream dessert. It contains more calories in a single serving than we should eat in a whole day, but our gut tells us to go with the brownie instead of the fruit platter. Too often, we choose a dessert that we later regret (myself included).

In the ancient savanna, it was critical for humans to eat as much sugar as possible to survive. In the modern environment, our gut reactions still pull us to do so, despite the harm caused by eating too many brownies. Simply knowing the drawbacks is insufficient protection. I'll admit that cheesecake is my Achilles' heel, although I've gotten much better at making wiser decisions—in my eating, business, and other life areas—using the strategies described in this book.

Making a business decision based on gut reactions comes from the same impulse as eating brownies instead of fruit, even though the business decision might have more devastating consequences. However, unlike the extensive research-based public messages regarding our health, we have only recently started to discover and popularize research about how to manage our intuitions around business decision-making to ensure the health of our businesses and careers.

You might convince yourself that you've made a lot of good decisions when you follow your gut. Unfortunately, the term *gut reaction* is used broadly in business contexts to refer to all sorts of internal impulses. This excessively fuzzy concept spans both very useful and trustworthy habits you developed for making quality decisions on the job as well as dangerous intuitions and instincts from our ancestors. As a leader, you might have learned counterintuitive behaviors to delegate tasks effectively and avoid micromanaging, or how to glance quickly at a department's profit and loss statement and recognize what needs to be addressed, or hear a sales pitch and immediately evaluate whether it's a good fit for your needs.

Your decisions might be quick, intuitive, and accurate, and it might feel like you're going with your gut. However, remember that these are acquired skills for which you had to learn to do the right thing rather than trust your instincts, just like you learned to drive a car and can now do so automatically.

Our minds can't tell the difference between our natural, primitive, and often dangerous instincts and our learned, civilized, and effective decision-making impulses. It can feel just as intuitive and comfortable to grab another brownie as to decide which sales pitch to consider and which to ignore. That's why business leaders should never trust their instincts and intuitions or go with their gut. Instead, you should evaluate to see if this internal impulse comes from a place of extensive experience from which you learned to make correct decisions; if so, trust that instinct. If it comes from elsewhere, such as, "This just doesn't feel right" or "This just feels right," the gut reaction might be one of the many dangerous judgment errors we all make as human beings. Verify whether this gut reaction points to a business threat or opportunity, instead of going with your heart and following your instincts on a business decision.

Studies from behavioral economics, psychology, cognitive neuroscience, and related fields reveal the many types of dangerous judgment errors—what scholars term *cognitive biases*—that we make in business and other areas. More importantly, the last few years have witnessed cutting-edge findings in *debiasing*—the practice of reducing or eliminating cognitive biases—that provide us with many new techniques to address dangerous judgment errors in our professional lives.

Unfortunately, popularizing this research is very difficult, at least in business contexts. Unscrupulous actors in the food industry are feeding us as many empty calories as they can for the sake of profit, despite the tragic consequences to our health and research showing the dangers of eating such unhealthy food. Similarly, powerful business gurus have built their careers by claiming that we should follow our guts regardless of the catastrophic consequences for our profits. Fearing for their livelihoods, they rail against hard-nosed, research-based business advice about distrusting our intuitions.

I hope you would fire your personal trainer if they told you to eat caramel brownies instead of fruit. Unfortunately, no business consultant, coach, speaker, author, or other expert is afraid of being fired for telling you to follow your gut.

The opposition of prominent business gurus to this paradigm shift is a major reason why this is the first book to focus on cognitive biases in business leadership and how we can fight these cognitive biases effectively. Don't believe me? Google it, and you'll see that although there are plenty of books on cognitive biases, none of them offer a book-length deep dive on understanding and solving the problems they cause for our businesses and careers.

I've lost count of business book publishers who told me that they like my writing style and find the mounds of research convincing, but would not publish this book. They claim they want to avoid books that directly contradict the popular business authors they work with for whom "follow your gut" is a central message. Other writers who follow a research-based approach to gut reactions experience similar challenges.

I self-published several books, most notably the bestselling *The Truth-Seeker's Handbook* (available on Amazon), which focuses on evaluating reality clearly in different areas of our lives, business and otherwise, to arrive at the best decisions. However, self-published books don't have major reach and don't offer much credibility. I'm deeply grateful that Career Press decided to take a risk and publish this book, despite the strong headwinds.

You should read this book if you're an executive in a Fortune 500 company, a small business owner, or a nonprofit executive director who wants to lead your organization safely and securely into the increasingly disrupted future and avoid the trip wires that will cause your competitors to stumble. You should read this book if you're an HR leader or midlevel manager in a large or midsize business that wants to improve internal processes, improve employee engagement, reduce unhelpful team conflicts, improve teamwork, and cultivate a flourishing internal culture in your organization, team, or unit. You should read this book if you're a future leader and want to guide your supervisors to make the best decisions for your organization. You should read this book if you're a professional who wants to avoid disastrous judgment errors in managing your present and future career.

If you know any such folks, give them a copy of this book; it will be the best gift you can give them in regard to their businesses and careers. Given they read it and apply these strategies, it will mark a paradigm shift in their professional lives. You should especially give it to them if they believe they are immune to dangerous judgment errors. That belief is one of the most dangerous cognitive biases, called the ***bias blind spot,*** which tends to impact successful people the most.[1] As the Bible says in Proverbs 16:18, "Pride goeth before destruction, and a haughty spirit before a fall."

About Me

My deep passion about this topic, as well as a streak of determination (some might say stubbornness), makes me willing to be a maverick and take on entrenched interests in pushing for a counterintuitive, research-based, data-driven paradigm shift to improve business health. This passion is personal.

As a kid, my dad told me with utmost conviction and absolutely no reservation to "go with your gut." I ended up making some really bad decisions in my professional activities, which included wasting several years of my life pursuing a medical career. I also watched him follow his gut and make some terrible choices that harmed my family, such as hiding some of his salary from my mom for several years. After she discovered this and several other financial secrets he kept, her trust was broken, which was a major factors that led to their prolonged separation; fortunately, they eventually reconciled, but the lack of trust could never be fully repaired.

My conviction that the omnipresent advice to "follow your gut" was hollow grew stronger as I came of age around the turn of the millennium during the dotcom boom and bust, and the fraudulent accounting scandals. Seeing prominent business leaders blow through hundreds of millions in online-based businesses without effective revenue streams (Webvan, *Boo.com, Pets.com*) was sobering, especially as I witnessed the hype that convinced investors to follow their intuitions and put money into dotcoms. At the same time, I learned about how the top executives of Enron, Tyco, and World-Com used illegal accounting practices to scam investors. Since it was inevitable that their crimes would be discovered and eventually lead to ruined reputations and long jail sentences, the best explanation for their irrational behavior came from their willingness to follow their guts.

Later, I read with sadness (but no surprise) in Paul Carroll and Chunka Mui's *Billion Dollar Lessons* that, in 46 percent of the 423 American companies with assets totaling more than $500 million that filed for bankruptcy between 1981 and 2007, the causes of bankruptcy could have been avoided if the leaders had made wiser strategy judgments (read: where the leaders did not follow their guts).[2] In many of the remaining 53 percent, better decisions would have substantially reduced the problems and likely prevented bankruptcy. Poor strategic leadership decision-making is responsible for such disasters, yet neither these leaders nor their followers received professional development in making decisions, despite the abundance of evidence that it's easy to improve one's judgment skills.

It was especially depressing for me to read the accounts of employees, stockholders, and communities devastated by the bankruptcies, especially in cases such as Enron, where the corporate leaders encouraged their employees to buy stocks while the leaders themselves were selling as the company danced on the brink of disaster. On a smaller but much more widespread scale, according to the US Small Business Administration, about half of all small businesses fail within the first five years.[3] The decisions made by their owners explain much of why they failed.

As someone with an ethical code of utilitarianism—desiring the most good for the largest number—I felt a calling to reduce suffering and improve well-being through helping business leaders and professionals avoid dangerous judgment errors. Therefore, while I pursued a doctorate that focused on decision-making in historical settings at the University of North Carolina at Chapel Hill, and later taught as a tenure-track professor in Ohio State University's Decision Sciences Collaborative and History Department, I also started to popularize these topics outside of academia. Eventually, I shifted away from academia to devote my full-time efforts to consulting, coaching, speaking, and writing as the CEO of the boutique consulting and training firm Disaster Avoidance Experts *(www.DisasterAvoidanceExperts.com)*. Our clients range from mid-size businesses and nonprofits to Fortune 500 companies such as Aflac, Fifth Third Bank, Honda, IBM, and Nationwide Insurance. With this book, you can get an in-depth look into the methods and techniques for which such clients paid five and six figures.

My paradigm-shifting content was featured in more than 400 articles I wrote and more than 350 interviews I gave to popular venues that include *Fast Company, CBS News, Time, Scientific American, Psychology Today, The Conversation, Business Insider, Government Executive, Inc. Magazine*, and CNBC. You might have learned about this book from one of them. If you liked the style of one or more of those mainstream venues, you will like the engaging and absorbing style of this book.

Moreover, there are three things that I can promise you about the book's content. These three commitments are based on more than two decades of my work in consulting, coaching, and speaking, while conducting my own research as well as reading studies by others on how to avoid dangerous judgment errors.

First, if you read thoroughly, do the exercises, and apply the strategies to your organization, you can feel secure that you will avoid a host of potential disasters, and you will be empowered to seize unexpected opportunities. This puts you head and shoulders above your competitors and will maximize your bottom line. Second, you will be truly confident and sleep soundly knowing that you will exceed expectations for everyone around you because you won't fall into cognitive biases. Third, you will experience a decrease in stress and anxiety during your workday because you substantially improved your relationships with coworkers and other business collaborators.

If you are in a leadership position, and/or in a position to influence your organization's professional development and training policies, you get the additional benefit of greatly improving your team and organization when you bring them this knowledge. Discounts are available on bulk orders of the book (contact *Info@DisasterAvoidanceExperts.com*), and the exercises in the book are excellent for group-based professional development. Likewise, you can use this information to inform and improve your organization's business system and internal processes, subtly shaping the decision-making structure to minimize dangerous judgment errors.

What you will not find in this book is unethical strategies, such as how to most effectively exploit your employees or manipulate your customers. Sure, behavioral economics research can be used for these unethical purposes, and unfortunately some scholar-practitioners (whom I won't name) sell expertise on how to do so. My sense of ethics around preventing suffering and improving well-being and my commitment to integrity does not permit me to offer such advice, and you won't find any in this book or other offerings from Disaster Avoidance Experts.

Eight-Step Decision-Making Model

It is tragic that business leaders consider making the best decisions as the key hallmark of business success, yet they treat the process of decision-making as something intuitive and almost magical, to be acquired only by hard-earned experience or possessed by a select few genius CEOs who deserve a top-notch pay package. The reality is that a first-rate decision-making process is teachable and learnable, and it boils down to an eight-step model for any significant decision. Unfortunately, the leaders of small, midsize, and large businesses and nonprofits often skip critical steps of the model, leading them to the fate of the bankrupt companies discussed by Carroll and Mui.

1. IDENTIFY THE NEED FOR A DECISION TO BE MADE.

Such recognition bears particular weight when there's no explicit crisis that cries out for a decision or when your intuition make it uncomfortable to acknowledge the need for a tough decision. The best decision-makers take initiative to recognize the need for decisions before they become an emergency, and they don't let gut reactions cloud their decision-making capacity.

2. Gather relevant information from a variety of informed perspectives on the issue at hand.

Value especially those opinions with which you disagree, because they empower you to distance yourself from the comfortable reliance on your gut instincts and help you recognize potential bias blind spots.

3. Decide on the goals you want to reach, and paint a clear vision of the desired outcome.

Use the data from step two to accomplish this step. It is particularly important to recognize when a seemingly one-time decision is a symptom of an underlying issue with processes and practices. Address these root problems as part of the outcome you want to achieve.

4. Develop clear decision-making criteria to evaluate options.

These criteria will show you how to get to your vision.

5. Generate viable options that can achieve your goals.

We frequently fall into the trap of generating insufficient options to make the best decisions, especially for solving underlying challenges, so it's important to generate more options than seems intuitive to us. Also remember that this is a brainstorming step, so don't judge options, even though they might seem outlandish or politically unacceptable. In my experience, the optimal choice often involves elements drawn from out-of-the-box and innovative options.

6. Weigh these options and pick the best of the bunch.

Mix and match parts of different options as seems best suited to the situation at hand. When weighing options, beware of going with your initial preferences, and try to see your preferred choice in a harsh light. Moreover, separate the option from the person who presented the option to minimize the impact of personalities, relationships, and internal politics on the decision.

7. IMPLEMENT THE OPTION YOU CHOSE.

Before and during the process of implementation, consider how your decision can go wrong and guard against these failures. Most importantly, ensure clear accountability and communication around the decision's enactment.

8. EVALUATE THE IMPLEMENTATION PROCESS AND REVISE AS NEEDED.

Note that you'll often go back and forth among these steps. Doing so is an inherent part of making a significant decision, and it does not indicate a problem in your process. For example, say you're at the option-generation stage, and you discover relevant new information. You might need to go back and revise the goals and criteria stages.

Unfortunately, dangerous judgment errors at any stage can cause disasters for businesses and careers. If we flinch away from unpleasant information—a typical problem in the business settings discussed in this book—we may not sense that a decision needs to be made. We'll wind up like Kodak, whose leadership ignored very clear evidence that digital cameras were gaining ground in the 1990s but chose to remain aboard the sinking ship of photographic film, resulting in its 2012 bankruptcy. Perhaps we'll make the all-too-common mistake of failing to generate sufficient options. This error happens in situations where CEOs are fired a short time after being hired, which is good evidence that the board of directors failed to consider a strong enough slate of candidates. John Flannery served as CEO of General Electric for just over a year, from August 2017 to October 2018, before being ousted. Maybe we'll fail to weigh options wisely and make a bad mistake, such as when Time Warner merged with a greatly overvalued AOL in 2000 for $165 billion, the largest merger in history at that time. When the dotcom bubble burst shortly after the merger, it decreased AOL stock from a valuation of $226 billion down to about $20 billion.

This book focuses, not only on the cognitive biases that can derail us at any stage of the decision-making process, but also on how we can resolve these issues. If you're in a crunch time right now and lack the time needed to read the whole book before making important decisions, then read the latter part of Chapter 1, which offers a series of applicable techniques. If you don't have time for that, and need a super-quick tactic right now, here's something you can use immediately: five questions you should ask about any decision to minimize dangerous judgment errors and maximize the likelihood of making the best decision and implementing it well. You should also think about these questions as you go through the eight-step decision-making model outlined on pages 13–15.

Five Questions to Avoid Decision Disasters

1. WHAT IMPORTANT INFORMATION DIDN'T I YET FULLY CONSIDER?

A common danger involves looking only for evidence that supports your preferred option, so look twice as hard for evidence that goes against it. Another aspect of important information means generating sufficient options to find the best option, as opposed to taking a mental shortcut by settling on the first attractive option. Find at least five highly attractive options to help you make a wise choice. At the same time, you want to avoid gathering too much information and getting stuck in what's known as "analysis paralysis." Focus on gathering only truly important information. Ideally, you should take time to consider what kind of information is truly important before making the decision, so that you don't have to make that determination in the heat of the moment during the decision-making process.

2. WHAT RELEVANT DANGEROUS JUDGMENT ERRORS DIDN'T I YET ADDRESS?

There are many different kinds of cognitive biases, some more relevant than others to specific kinds of decisions. This book will guide you to understand the most significant ones for business settings; for a very quick and rough overview, check out the assessment in Chapter 7, specifically the section that discusses the biases that commonly harm businesses.

3. WHAT WOULD A TRUSTED AND OBJECTIVE ADVISER SUGGEST I DO?

I hope you have mentors, coaches, consultants, and other experts to whom you can turn to help you make a good decision. Decisions that we make by ourselves or in small groups with a powerful leader lead businesses and careers into the dust. By now, you know to beware of advisers who tell you to trust your instincts, follow your intuition, and be authentic. If you don't have anyone to ask, try to imagine what a trusted and objective adviser might tell you; doing so can have a positive impact on your decision-making outcomes and lead you to recognize some biased mental patterns.

4. HOW HAVE I ADDRESSED THE WAYS IT COULD FAIL?

This question is a transition from the decision-making stage regarding which option to choose into implementing that option to achieve your goals. Indeed, if you chose the best available option but dropped the ball on implementation, you're not going to reach your goals. This question helps to ensure you will achieve your envisioned outcome. Although you're mostly settled on your choice, and you're thinking about the challenge of what happens when the rubber hits the road, be ready to rethink the option if you discover truly momentous obstacles in enactment. Sometimes, as you evaluate how you're going to implement it, the option that appears best on your initial decision-making criteria doesn't work, and then it's time to go back and revisit earlier stages with this new information.

5. WHAT NEW INFORMATION WOULD CAUSE ME TO REVISIT THE DECISION?

I've seen business leaders weighed down by bitter attacks of self-doubt about a decision they made. I've also observed teams of executives fight after a decision is made, with those who preferred a different option criticizing any sign that the chosen option has problems, even ones anticipated from the beginning. To avoid these scenarios, and to provide you and your team with the ability to focus your full attention and energy on implementation, you need to avoid reconsidering the decision whenever any potentially relevant data pops up. Take time to evaluate what new information—including quality and quantity—would cause you to revisit the decision. For instance, you can set a financial trigger ($30 million in sales), a survey trigger (15 percent increase in customer satisfaction), a prospect trigger (thirty new prospect meetings within the next six months), or a combination of any of these as a means of evaluating whether it's time to revisit the decision. In short, answering this question in advance will help you down the road.

Although you would benefit from using these five questions for any decision, reading the rest of the book will provide you with the true in-depth immersion to avoid dangerous judgment errors that have previously been available only to my consulting, coaching, and speaking clients. Chapter 1 provides a broad overview of the latest research on how we think and feel in business settings, and the specific techniques we can use to address dangerous judgment errors. The subsequent five chapters go through the thirty or so cognitive biases that hold the most threat for business decision-making and offer concrete solutions for each of these problems. The final chapter provides an assessment tool to evaluate yourself and your team, which enables you to adapt the information in the book to your own business context and take the necessary steps to address any problems you may discover.

Throughout, the hard science that backs up the dangerous judgment errors is made relevant to business settings mainly through stories of my consulting, coaching, and speaking clients, as well as famous business case studies from the United States and around the globe. I focus on stories from my clients (without naming specific names or organizations) because I know intimately the kind of challenges that they experienced and how they resolved them, or failed to do so. I also share several stories of my own failures and successes in addressing dangerous judgment errors. Hey, no one is perfect, and I never claimed to be. Many more materials relevant to the book, such as worksheets, manuals, and a digital version of the assessment, can be found at *www.DisasterAvoidanceExperts.com/NeverGut* and you can sign up at *www.DisasterAvoidanceExperts.com/Newsletter* to receive additional resources on this topic.

It is my fervent hope that you can learn from the experiences and research presented here to reduce suffering and improve well-being for yourself, your employees, your investors, and your communities through protecting and maximizing your bottom line. I'm eager to hear about your experiences. Please write me at *Gleb@DisasterAvoidanceExperts.com.* Now, take the next steps to making the best decisions for your business and career by diving into the book!

Chapter 1

The Gut or the Head?

Chapter Key Benefits

✿ Identify the systematic and predictable situations in which we are most likely to make bad business decisions by understanding how our brain is wired.

✿ Learn the principles and broad strategy behind effective tactical techniques to prevent poor decisions.

✿ Discover twelve cutting-edge tactical techniques used by pioneering business leaders to address dangerous judgment errors in their everyday business environment.

Many pundits heap praise on those leaders who make quick gut decisions about the direction of their company, about whether to launch a new product, or about which candidate to hire. Sadly, going with our gut frequently leads to devastating results for our professional lives, as I saw in news headlines that were relevant as I finished up this book.

In May 2017, hackers stole the credit information of more than 148 million people from the consumer credit reporting company Equifax. The data breach exploited a security flaw that the company should have known it needed to fix. It was called "entirely preventable" by a December 2018 Congressional Report by the House Oversight Committee.[1] Even worse, the Equifax C-suite decided to cover up the incident for several months. The disastrous decision to conduct a cover-up—inevitably discovered later—gravely damaged Equifax's reputation, caused a large and lasting drop in the company's stock, and led to the CEO and a number of other top executives being forced out due to incompetence.

John Schnatter, the founder of Papa John's, sued the company after it forced him out for using a racial epithet. When he testified against the company during a court hearing on October 1, 2018, he described a "gut feeling" that the board of directors sought actively to push him out and accused the board of breaching its fiduciary duties.[2] This was terrible PR for the company, which brings down its stock and sales, and it hurts Schnatter as well because he holds a 30 percent stake in the company.

What about Elon Musk's infamous tweet on August 7, 2018, when he said he was considering taking Tesla private and has funding secured for a buyout per share at $420 (a code for marijuana)? The tweet led to an SEC investigation and settlement. Musk gave up his role as chair of the board while remaining CEO; Musk and Tesla each paid $20 million in fines, and Tesla appointed more independent directors to the board.[3] Tesla's stock fell dramatically during this incident.

Make no mistake: each of the example cases exemplify value-destroying decisions that hurt shareholders because top corporate leaders followed their gut. By the time you hold this book in your hands, I'm confident more breaking headlines will illustrate the foolishness of corporate leaders going with their intuitions instead of evaluating reality to make wise decisions.

These examples of top leaders at prominent companies are not isolated incidences: a four-year study by *LeadershipIQ.com* interviewed 1,087 board members from 286 organizations that forced out their chief executive officers. It found that more than 20 percent of CEOs got fired for denying reality, meaning they refused to recognize negative facts about the organization's performance.[4] Other research shows that professionals at all levels suffer from the tendency to deny uncomfortable facts in business settings.[5]

The scope of this problem became crystal clear to me in graduate school when I started to study the kind of errors human beings make when we trust our gut. At the time, I was doing some teaching as a graduate student. At the end of my first semester of teaching, my supervisor called me into his office and gave me some constructive criticism about my performance.

He was somewhat rough and forceful in his delivery of the criticism. Perhaps he didn't need to say "lily-livered coward" when he described what he perceived as the excessively high scores I gave my students. Naturally, I felt very grateful for his advice and thanked him immediately and profusely . . . NOT!

What I really wanted to do was deny his criticism: shout back at him, tell him he was wrong, and say that his grading system sucked. That's what my gut was telling me to do. My face turned bright red and I clenched my fists, as my gut was also telling me to pop him one.

It took everything I had to restrain myself, dial down my emotions, and stop from yelling back or doing something worse. I wouldn't have had much of a career in academia—or anywhere—if I couldn't do it. Through a haze of red, I told him I'd do what he wanted with the grading system, and slunk out of his office with a scowl on my face and my fists clenching and unclenching. I ended up changing my grading style to suit his preferences. He was my boss, after all, and I wanted the teaching gig.

What did you do when you received constructive criticism—well delivered or rough—from your boss, your customer, your colleague, or your coach? What did your gut tell you to do in that moment? Did it tell you to be aggressive and shout back? Perhaps it told you to hunker down and disengage. Maybe it pushed you to put your fingers in your ears and sing, "La-la-la, I can't hear you!"

Behavioral scientists call these three types of responses the *fight-flight-freeze response.* You might have heard about it as the saber-toothed tiger response, which means the system our brain evolved to deal with threats in our ancestral savanna environment. This response stems from the older parts of our brain, such as the amygdala, which developed early in our evolutionary process.

I Feel, Therefore I Am

Fight-flight-freeze forms a central part of one of the two systems of thinking that (roughly speaking) determine our mental processes. It's not the old Freudian model of the id, the ego, and the super-ego, which has been phased out by new research on the topic.[6] One of the main scholars in this field is Daniel Kahneman, who won the Nobel Prize for his research on behavioral economics. He calls the two systems of thinking System 1 and System 2, but I think *autopilot system* and *intentional system* describe these systems more clearly.[7]

The autopilot system corresponds to our emotions and intuitions; that's where we get the fight-flight-freeze response. This system guides our daily habits, helps us make snap decisions, and reacts instantly to dangerous life-and-death situations. Although it helped our survival in the past, the fight-flight-freeze response is not a great fit for many aspects of modern life. We have many small stresses that are not life threatening, but the autopilot system treats them as saber-toothed tigers. Doing so produces an unnecessarily stressful everyday life experience that undermines our mental and physical well-being.

Moreover, the snap judgments that result from intuitions and emotions usually feel "true" because they are fast and powerful, and we feel comfortable when we go with them. The decisions that arise from our gut reactions are often right, especially in situations that resemble the ancient savanna. Unfortunately, our modern business environments don't have much in common with the savanna, and with the increase in technological disruption—ranging from teleconferences to social media—the office of the future will look even less like our ancestral environment. The autopilot system will therefore lead us astray more and more, in systematic and predictable ways.

The intentional system reflects rational thinking and centers around the prefrontal cortex, the part of the brain that evolved more recently. According to research, it developed as humans started to live within larger social groups.[8] This thinking system helps us handle more complex mental activities, such as managing individual and group relationships, logical reasoning, abstract thinking, evaluating probabilities, and learning new information, skills, and habits.

Whereas the automatic system requires no conscious effort to function, the intentional system is mentally tiring and requires a deliberate effort to turn on. With enough motivation and appropriate training, the intentional system can turn on in situations where the autopilot system makes systematic and predictable errors.

The following is a quick visual comparison of the two systems:

Autopilot System	Intentional System
⇒ Fast, intuitive, emotional self	⇒ Conscious, reasoning, mindful self
⇒ Requires no effort	⇒ Takes intentional effort to turn on and drains mental energy
⇒ Automatic thinking, feeling, and behavior habits	⇒ Used mainly when we learn new information and use reason and logic
⇒ Mostly makes good decisions, but is prone to some predictable and systematic errors	⇒ Can be trained to turn on when it detects the autopilot system making errors

We tend to think of ourselves as rational thinkers when we use the intentional system. Unfortunately, that's not the case.

Scholars of this topic, such as Chip and Dan Health, compare the autopilot system to an elephant. It's by far the more powerful and predominant of the two systems because our emotions can often overwhelm our rationality. Moreover, our intuition and habits dominate the majority of our life; we're usually in autopilot mode. That's not a bad thing, as it would be mentally exhausting to think through every action and decision.

The intentional system is like the elephant's rider. It can guide the elephant to go in a direction that matches our goals. Certainly, the elephant part of the brain is huge and unwieldy, slow to turn and change, and stampedes at threats. But we can train the elephant. Your rider can become an elephant whisperer. Over time, you can use the intentional system to change your automatic thinking, feeling, and behavior patterns to avoid dangerous judgment errors.

It's crucial to recognize that these two systems of thinking are counterintuitive. They don't align with our conscious self-perception. Our mind feels like a cohesive whole. Unfortunately, this self-perception is simply a comfortable myth that helps us make it through the day. There is no actual "there"; our sense of self is a construct that results from multiple complex mental processes within the autopilot and intentional systems.

It will take a bit of time to incorporate this realization into your mental model of yourself and others—in other words, how you perceive your mind to work. The bottom line is that you're not who you think you are. The conscious, self-reflective part of you is like a little rider on top of that huge elephant of emotions and intuitions.

Do you want to see what the tension between the autopilot system and the intentional system feels like in real life? Think back to the last time your supervisor, client, or investor gave you constructive critical feedback. How easy was it to truly listen and take in the information, instead of defending yourself and your work? That feeling is your willpower trying to get the intentional system to override the cravings of the autopilot system.[9]

Consider the last flame war you got into online, or perhaps an in-person argument with your loved one. Did the flame war or in-person argument solve things? Did you manage to convince the other person? I'd be surprised if it did. Arguments usually don't lead to anything beneficial. Often, even if you win the argument, you end up harming relationships you care about.

Looking back, you probably regret at least some of the flame wars or in-person arguments in which you've engaged. You might wonder why you engaged in the first place. It's the old fight response coming to the fore, without you noticing it. Unlike that situation with my boss, or when you were getting some constructive critical feedback, it's not immediately obvious that a fight response will hurt you down the road. Thus, you let the elephant go rogue, and it stampeded all over the place.

Whether in personal or business settings, letting the elephant loose is like allowing a bull into a china shop. Broken dishes will be the least of your problems. Scholars use the term *akrasia* to refer to situations in which we act against our better judgment. In other words, we act irrationally, defined in behavioral science as going against our own self-reflective goals.

But My Gut Has Helped Make Many Good Decisions!

Let's make sure we're talking about the same thing here. Remember that the term *gut reaction* is used too broadly. It covers both helpful learned behaviors that have become automatic as well as dangerous, savanna-based impulses. In your professional life, you acquire many healthy and helpful tendencies in situations where you get quick and accurate feedback on your judgments. As a result, you develop excellent decision-making skills in a specific area. Remember: we can't tell the difference between an internal feeling of comfort around such automatic civilized behaviors and the same intuitive sense of "rightness" around dangerous, primitive savanna instincts. Our brain processes them in the same autopilot system, and they feel the same to us. To differentiate, you need to check with your head before you decide whether the impulse comes from a trustworthy automatic learned behavior or an untrustworthy savanna intuition.

Research, coupled with my own experience, shows that in some instances savanna instincts can be helpful in business decision-making contexts; in other words, it's not necessarily irrational to follow your gut.[10] The limited number of situations in the modern world that correspond to the savanna environment result in mostly accurate signals from our primitive instincts. For example, in the savanna environment, we lived in tribes and had to rely on our gut reactions to evaluate fellow tribal members. So if you have a long-standing business relationship with someone, and then you experience negative gut responses about their behavior in a new business deal, it's time to double-check the fine print. The same goes for employees: one of my clients caught his long-time CFO stealing after my client noticed unusual behavior changes in the CFO with no underlying cause.

However, don't buy into the myth that you can tell lies from truths. Studies show that we are very bad at distinguishing falsehoods from accurate statements. On average, we only detect 54 percent of lies, a shocking statistic considering we'd get 50 percent if we used random chance.[11]

Overall, it's never a good idea to go with your gut. Even in cases where you think you can rely on your intuition, it's best to use your instincts as a warning sign of potential danger and evaluate the situation analytically. For example, the person with whom you have a long business relationship might have just gotten some bad news, and their demeanor caused your instincts to misread the situation. Your extensive experience in a given topic might bring you to ruin if the market context changes and you use your old intuitions in a different environment, like a fish out of water.

Danger Zone: Cognitive Biases

Irrational behavior usually results from systematic and predictable mental errors that researchers term *cognitive biases*. Many of these systematic and predictable judgment errors stem from our evolutionary heritage because they helped us survive in the savanna environment, such as overreacting to the presence of a perceived threat. It was more beneficial to our survival to jump at 100 shadows than fail to jump at one saber-toothed tiger.

We are the descendants of those people who were evolutionarily selected for jumping at shadows. Of course, most cognitive biases do not serve us well in our modern environment, just like many mental habits we learned as children don't serve us well as adults.

Cognitive biases are also the result of inherent limitations in our mental processing capacities, such as our difficulty keeping track of many varied data points. This challenge results in formulas outperforming experts in typical situations, such as evaluating the credit worthiness of loan applicants. The best systems combine formulas for typical situations with expert analysis of outliers.

Most cognitive biases result from mistakes made by going with our gut reactions, meaning autopilot system errors. More rarely, cognitive biases are associated with intentional system errors. As you can see from the previous argument example, you may have used reason and logic to win the argument, but in the end, you behaved irrationally by harming yourself if cultivating the relationship was more important to you than winning the argument.

Research has found more than 100 cognitive biases that cause us to make terrible decisions.[12] Cognitive biases fall into four broad categories: inaccurate evaluations of oneself, evaluations of others, strategic evaluations of risks and rewards, and tactical evaluations in project implementation.

Throughout the book, I'll give tentative evolutionary explanations for a number of biases that reflect plausible scenarios for how they might have resulted from our evolutionary heritage based on my reading of the current scientific literature. It's quite possible that these explanations will be updated and changed by newer findings, and not all scholars will fully agree with my interpretations. That's what it means to read research that's on the cutting edge, instead of staid textbooks that contain research a generation or two out of date.

So that's bad news, right? Our minds are messed up. We're screwed. End of play, curtain down, you can go home now. But wait, there's more! Not all hope is lost. Our intentional system can be trained to spot situations in which we're likely to make mistakes because of cognitive biases and correct them, because the latter are systematic and predictable.

I'm not saying it's easy, as doing so involves building up a series of mental habits, many of which you might not have right now. If you want easy, you can put this book down and go watch some TV to make sure you keep up with the Kardashians. You'll see some great models of rational behavior there, I'm sure. (My editor asked me to clarify that the previous statement was sarcasm, in case anyone missed it. I doubt readers of this book would miss sarcasm, but editors are editors.)

If you want to avoid disasters in your business life, you need to put in some effort. No pain, no gain, right? Developing the mental habits described in this book is like going to gym for your mind. If you want good physical health, go to the gym. If you want to have a healthy business, read books on making wise decisions. Do the exercises in the books that teach you how to apply these strategies to your business and career, and then go and apply them.

What can be more important than improving your business decisions? Success in our professional lives is determined by the decisions we make every day. If you screw up these decisions, don't expect to have the kind of financial outcomes that you want and deserve.

Not what you hoped to hear? Here's something more hopeful. You'll be cheered by the fact that the strategies outlined in the following pages all come from research in behavioral economics, psychology, cognitive neuroscience, and other disciplines that investigate how to debias cognitive biases.[13] *Debiasing* in this context does not specifically refer to "bias" the way you're used to hearing this term (racism, sexism, and so on). Instead, debiasing solves the kind of cognitive biases that lead to devastating consequences for our decision-making. You also get more than two decades of my experience in consulting, coaching, and speaking on this topic to business and nonprofit leaders as the CEO of Disaster Avoidance Experts. I will show you how pioneering leaders and organizations apply debiasing strategies to their everyday business contexts.

Twelve Techniques to Address Dangerous Judgment Errors

Let's discuss twelve specific debiasing methods in the workplace:

1. Identify and make a plan to address dangerous judgment errors.
2. Delay decision-making.
3. Mindfulness meditation.
4. Probabilistic thinking.
5. Make predictions about the future.
6. Consider alternative explanations and options.
7. Consider past experiences.
8. Consider long-term future and repeating scenarios.
9. Consider other people's perspectives.
10. Use an outside view to get an external perspective.
11. Set policy to guide your future self and organization.
12. Make a precommitment.

First of all, we need to *identify the various dangerous judgment errors that we are facing and make a plan to address them*.

Awareness of the problem is the first step to solving the problem. Sounds obvious, right? However, debiasing by learning about cognitive biases is trickier than it might seem. It would be wonderful if you could read a book or listen to a speech about these dangerous judgment errors and voila, you're cured!

It's not that easy. Research demonstrates that just finding out about a cognitive bias doesn't solve it. Instead, those who are learning about a cognitive bias have to evaluate where in their professional activities this mental error leads them astray and causes them pain, and then they need to make a specific plan to address the problem.

Why? Addressing the autopilot system requires inspiring strong emotions. Changing our habitual instincts is hard, and I mean *hard*. We have to really want to invest strong emotions into change because we dislike the current situation. To make that investment, it's critical for us to have personal buy-in for transforming our intuitions. Simply learning about the cognitive bias doesn't create such intense feelings. However, when we identify in a deep and thorough manner where that dangerous judgment error is truly hurting us—the critical pain points caused by these cognitive biases in our personal professional activities and in the teams and organizations we lead—it helps empower the strong negative emotions needed to go against our gut reactions.

Yet even that is not enough, just like it wouldn't be enough to strongly dislike our body weight without a tangible plan to get fit through changing our diet and exercise regimen. Make no mistake, the work you're about to do to become mentally fit is just as hard as the work required to make a drastic change in your physical health.

To help you address these dangerous judgment errors in your professional life, this book includes exercises during which you will self-reflect on where each cognitive bias causes problems for your bottom line and develop a plan to fix these issues. Reading the book without doing the exercise is like leaping halfway across a deep hole; you'll end up worse than you started. You'll be aware of the problem without solving it and end up suffering more than you would if you remained in blissful ignorance. So do yourself, your colleagues, your clients, your customers, and anyone else impacted by your professional activities the favor of completing the exercises to help avoid disasters in your business activities. Alternatively, the Kardashians await.

Doing these exercises will involve writing in your profession-al journal, whether a paper journal or electronic one. What? You don't have a professional journal?! How do you keep track of the brilliant ideas you have that will take sales to the next level or rock-et-boost the motivation of your employees? Where do you keep notes from all those workshops you attend?

Don't tell me scraps of paper. If you don't have a professional journal to capture your ideas, you are doing a huge disservice to yourself and your organization. Pause for a moment and set up a journaling system if you don't have one; it is truly the most im-portant thing you can do with your time right now.

You're back? Got the system up and running? Good.

A great deal of debiasing involves some form of shifting from the autopilot to the intentional mode of thinking. After all, the large majority (although not all) of the mental errors we tend to make come from our autopilot system. One of the simplest ways to do so is to *delay our reactions and decisions.* Remember how your mom told you to count to ten when you were angry? Well, it works! Now you can implement similar techniques to stop yourself from reacting on autopilot. Instead, give yourself the time and space needed to cool down and have a more reasoned, slower response to the situation.

Although counting to ten works for an immediate response situation—our intentional system takes a second or two to turn on, while the autopilot system takes only milliseconds—a more intense arousal response will require about twenty to thirty minutes to calm down. That is how long it takes our sympathetic nervous system, which is the system activated in fight-flight-freeze responses, to cool down through turning on our parasympathetic nervous system, also called the rest and digest system.

You won't be surprised by this next one: *mindfulness meditation.* Research finds that meditation treats numerous problems, from pain to anxiety; now, we know it also helps us address cognitive biases. Why? It is most likely due to a combination of delay, awareness, and focus. We are more capable of delaying unhelpful intuitive impulses, being more aware of when we are going with our gut, and focusing more on turning on our intentional system.

Our autopilot system does not do well with numbers. It's in essence a yes or no system, attraction or aversion, threat or opportunity. This black-and-white thinking can be solved through the intentional system approach of applying probabilistic estimates of reality. Also called *Bayesian reasoning,* after the creator of the Bayesian theorem Rev. Thomas Bayes, *probabilistic thinking* evaluates the probability of what reality looks like and updates your beliefs about the world as more information becomes available.

For instance, say your business partner said something hurtful; your intuitive response is to say something mean in response. A probabilistic thinking approach requires you to step back and evaluate the likelihood that your business partner *meant* to hurt you or whether a miscommunication occurred. You would then seek further evidence to help you update your beliefs about whether your business partner meant to hurt you or not.

As an example, if she is looking at the ledger for the month and says, "Wow, our electric bill is so high this month" and you like the office to be warm in the winter and set the thermostat high, it's easy to feel as though the comment is an attack on you and say something hurtful in response. For instance, if she hasn't brought in as much business as she usually does, a hurtful (and all-too-typical) response would be, "Well, we wouldn't have to worry about the size of the bill if we had more money coming in." Drama follows.

By contrast, probabilistic thinking has you evaluate the likelihood that she deliberately hurt you and you seek more evidence first before deciding how to respond. Thus, you might ask, "Are you concerned about the electricity costs of me setting the thermostat high?" Then, she can respond, "Well, the electric bill is about two times as high as last month, and you were running the thermostat then. I think the electric company just screwed up. I'll call them tomorrow." Team conflict averted, thanks to probabilistic thinking. (I had a version of this conversation with my business partner and wife, Agnes Vishnevkin, last winter)

My question to Agnes reflects an important aspect of probabilistic thinking: launching experiments to gain additional information. Because our gut reactions cause us to be vastly overconfident about what reality actually looks like, launching small experiments is a low-cost way to correct our evaluations of our business environment. Look for ways you can test out your theories, especially how to disprove them rather than confirm them, to address our tendencies to look only for information that supports our beliefs.

A key aspect of probabilistic thinking consists of using your existing knowledge about the likely shape of reality (called the *base rate probability,* also known as *prior probability*) to evaluate new evidence. In a keynote for a group of bank managers on using debiasing techniques to improve organizational performance, I spoke about using base rates to determine how to invest their time and energy into mentoring subordinates most effectively. In a facilitated exercise, I asked them to consider how their prior mentoring impacted their subordinates. Then, I asked them to compare the qualities of their current subordinates to the prior subordinates they mentored. Finally, I asked them to consider whether their mentoring energy was invested effectively compared to the impact they *could* have on subordinates.

Base rates here refer to their prior experience of investing energy into mentoring and the kind of outcomes they achieved. The discussion revealed that the current behavior of bank managers did not match their estimates of employee improvement. Overall, the managers were spending way too much time mentoring the worst performers—perhaps 70 percent of their time on average. Yet, the biggest impact of mentoring based on their prior experience came from improving the performance of their best performers. Informed by this evaluation of prior probabilities and how they compared to current actions, the managers decided to shift their mentoring energies and recommend that the worst performers get an outside coach, even if doing so would negatively impact their relationships with these employees.

A related strategy to probabilistic thinking involves ***making predictions about the future.*** For example, you think your customers will be pleased and more likely to provide more business and referrals if you send them holiday greeting cards. Combine making predictions with experimentation by testing out this hypothesis.

Select a holiday, say, Thanksgiving, and get some themed cards. Then, choose a batch of current customers that have comparable characteristics, for instance, independent financial advisers who have been customers between one and three years. Divide this group into two equal batches and send one batch greeting cards. Before doing so, predict the kind of outcomes you expect to see, such as a 10 percent boost in business and a 15 percent increase in referrals over the next three months. Then, see whether your prediction turns out to be true or not. Update your beliefs—and your business processes if sending greeting cards turns out to be a good investment—based on the outcomes of the experiment.

If you discuss the future in a team setting, making predictions goes along splendidly with making bets. Say you and your cofounder of a tech start-up disagree about how well the new round of financing will go. Make a bet of your own money—say $1,000—that angel investors will evaluate your company, for example, above or below a certain amount. Doing so is a terrific way to settle disagreements and prove who is best calibrated in evaluating reality accurately. There's something about putting down your own money that makes people step back and wake up a bit, especially if they are brimming with false confidence. The same sort of betting, perhaps for lower amounts, can be used to resolve questions in small businesses or lower levels of an organization.

The next debiasing strategy involves **considering alternative explanations and options.** Say your boss is curt with you at work. You might take this behavior as a sign that the boss is angry with you. You start to think about your past performance and analyze every aspect of it, and psych yourself out in a spiral of catastrophizing thinking. Debiasing in this case involves considering alternative explanations.

Perhaps your boss is in a bad mood because her lunch burrito didn't agree with her. Perhaps she's very busy, rushing to fulfill a customer's demands, and didn't have a chance to chat with you as she normally would. Numerous explanations exist for her behavior that do not involve being angry. When you combine considering the alternative with probabilistic thinking, you can follow up with your boss later in the day when she has a quiet moment and observe how she interacts with you. Then, update your beliefs based on this new interaction.

In general, try to find alternative evidence that would disconfirm your intuitive gut reaction to the situation. Next, make a fuller assessment based on additional evidence. It's crucial to decide in advance what kind of evidence would change your mind (or change the group's decision, if you're doing it as a team) before proceeding, so that you don't argue afterward about what evidence counts as "good enough."

In a group decision-making setting where two factions are at odds over which of two paths to take, you can get both to collaborate on evaluating what kind of evidence would need to be true for one of the paths to be the best course of action. Then, try to have both groups find disconfirming evidence that proves that path incorrect. That way, people won't fight each other, and instead will work alongside one another to problem-solve the issue at hand.

Likewise, expand the range of options you're considering through increasing your alternatives. For instance, you might be hesitant to hire someone because you're not sure he will be a good personality fit for your team, although he has the right skills on paper. Can you bring him on as a contractor for three months to see if he is a good fit before going through the process of hiring him full time?

Considering a wide range of alternative options is especially important in making substantial decisions. We have a great deal of research showing that everyone from executives to rank-and-file professionals tend to close off options too early and home in on a preferred choice. As a result, they make some real whoppers, ranging from career choices they regret to strategy decisions that cost companies billions of dollars. For example, an old media and new media company merger intended for heaven but destined for hell. (Yes, I'm looking at you, AOL and Time Warner.)

A very useful approach is to develop at least one and ideally two next best alternatives (NBAs) to your preferred option, and then look wide and deep for reasons you should go with one of the NBAs in a significant decision. The extra time and energy you spend doing so is worth the cost of making an awful choice and suffering a business disaster, as many of my clients told me after they started using this strategy compared to their prior decision-making processes that cost them dearly in the past.

Considering our past experiences also helps as a debiasing tactic. Are you always running late to work meetings? Are you the type of person who starts to get ready for a meeting that's fifteen minutes away exactly fifteen minutes before the meeting? Chronic lateness harms your relationships and reputation as well as your mental and physical well-being through constant elevated levels of cortisol, the stress hormone. Self-reflecting on how long activities have taken in the past to inform your current activities—for example, exactly when you should start to prepare for a meeting to be there with five minutes to spare—will help your business relationships and your well-being.

Considering past experience also involves reflecting on your past successes and applying them to the present. For instance, did you have your most successful sales calls when you took the time to prepare mentally to be in a positive mindset, researched the prospect extensively, and role-played what you would say? If so, then consider repeating the same strategy going forward.

Next, *evaluate the long-term future and repeating scenarios,* whether that means the long-term impact of a major decision or a series of repeating decisions that have a great long-term impact when combined. What happened the last time you asked your colleague to help you with a report by tomorrow? If he agreed, did he carry out his commitment, or just avoid you for the next couple of days and then pretend that nothing happened? Is this a pattern that repeats as you get increasingly aggravated about his failure?

If so, why ask him to help you in the first place? It's not like it will make the situation any better and will only cause more conflict and grief for you both. Maybe it's better to have a serious conversation with him about keeping his commitments or just let it slide. This kind of evaluation of repeating scenarios can greatly improve your business relationships.

Similarly, evaluate the long-term consequences of decisions. Ask yourself three questions: what do you expect the consequences of this decision to be a day from now? A month from now? A year from now? For instance, if you're anxious about cold-calling prospects regarding a new offer, what do you think will be the result of the cold-calling a day from now? Well, the anxiety would have faded, and you might have found a couple of people who are interested in your product. In a month, you might have made a sale to one of them. In a year, that person might be one of your best clients.

You probably heard the saying "Before you judge someone, walk a mile in their shoes." Turns out this approach, which means understanding other people's mental models and situational context, helps debiasing greatly. We tend to greatly underestimate the extent to which other people are different than we are. That's why the Golden Rule, do unto others as you would have them do unto you, is trumped by the Platinum Rule: do unto others as they would like to have done unto them. You'll get much better business outcomes if you practice the debiasing strategy of *considering other people's points of view* and focusing on their needs, not simply your own, in your interactions.

When was the last time you saw two of your colleagues arguing over something silly, perhaps lubricated by some alcohol in the evening after a conference? It happened to me a couple of days ago. From your outside perspective on the conflict, you recognize easily that fighting over the issue was not productive and even harmful. Why didn't they see it themselves? Because the inside view from within a situation blinds us to the broader context of what's going on, leading to poor decisions that harm our relationships. To help yourself address this problem, try to look at the situation as objectively as possible by **using an outside view to get an external perspective.**

The quickest but least reliable method is to get a quick external perspective from yourself. What you would recommend a peer do if the peer was in your position? You'll often have more clarity by gaining that distance from your own gut reactions and intuitions.

However, it's usually more effective to get an external perspective from other people, if at all possible. You can get this outside view by consulting an aggregator of external opinions. For instance, you can consult *Glassdoor.com,* which lists confidential reviews by employees about a company's culture and working conditions, before accepting a job at a company. You can also speak to someone you trust and who knows your quirks, including where you're likely to make mistakes.

It's especially helpful, whenever possible, to get that external perspective from someone with expertise on the topic. If you are challenged by managing two teams that are constantly at loggerheads with each other, go to someone in your organization who has successfully managed intransigent teams and get her advice. If you are struggling to address persistent personnel problems, such as lack of willingness to accept new initiatives, and you have no internal resources, consider getting an external consultant or coach to help.

One of the easiest ways to address cognitive biases involves **setting a policy that guides your future self or your organization.** In the heat of the moment it may be hard to delay decision-making, consider alternatives, or practice the Platinum Rule. Yet if you set a policy by which you abide, especially by using a decision aid, you can protect yourself from many dangerous biases. For example, say you committed to delay your responses to professional emails that make you mad for at least thirty minutes. That's a great policy, as it ensures you have enough time to cool down by turning on your parasympathetic nervous system through stepping away from the computer and taking a brief walk outside.

It would work even better with a decision aid, such as Gmail's "Undo Send" feature. If your autopilot system gets the better of you and you type out an angry response email and send it, the "Undo Send" feature allows you to unsend the email, at least for a few seconds after you hit "Send." That feature served me well a number of times (my default response in the saber-toothed scenario is fight). Other decision aids include creating checklists to consult on certain decisions or processes and making visible reminders to encourage us to be our best intentional selves. The eight-step decision-making model and the five key questions to avoid decision disasters described in the introduction are highly effective aids used widely by my clients, and printable versions of them are located on *www. DisasterAvoidanceExperts.com/NeverGut,* along with other resources for this book.

A critical aspect of setting a policy for your future self involves fighting against the anchoring bias, our tendency to be stuck excessive on our initial predispositions. Research strongly suggests that when we try to fight our intuitions, we tend to not go nearly as far as we should due to the anchoring bias. We need to go much further than feels comfortable to de-anchor ourselves and end up much closer to the best place to be. Don't worry, it is unlikely you will overshoot and go too far, according to the research. Setting a policy helps us go beyond our comfort zones.

For an organization, setting a policy is a standard matter. You can integrate all of the techniques described here—especially the decision-making model and the five key questions—as a central part of any decision-making process in your team or the organization as a whole. Likewise, throughout the book you'll see case studies of my clients adapting various policies into their organizations to fix problems caused by cognitive biases. Once these techniques are integrated into the business system and become part of the normal order of operations they protect the bottom lines of organizations.

A related strategy involves ***making a precommitment,*** especially a public commitment, to a certain set of behaviors, with an associated accountability mechanism. For instance, a business that joins the

Better Business Bureau commits to follow a set of ethical guidelines. This public promise, along with the BBB accountability mechanism, makes us more likely to follow that set of ethics, even when our autopilot system tempts us to take ethical shortcuts. The Pro-Truth Pledge (at *www.ProTruthPledge.org*) functions similarly for a public commitment to truthfulness for individual professionals, with a similar accountability mechanism. Both of these public commitments boost the reputation of a business or individual professional in exchange for being held accountable for one's promise. The autopilot system's tendency to cut corners is held in check (at least somewhat) by this commitment.

The public nature of a commitment encourages our community—the people who know about the commitment and care about helping us be our best selves—to support our efforts to change our behavior. Let's say that you have a weakness of saying yes too often to requests from your colleagues, and your boss is warning you that you're spread too thin and not getting your own work done. This happened to someone I was asked to coach. What I advised him to do—and he successfully implemented—was share this problem with the same colleagues who made requests for his help. They were highly supportive, both decreasing their requests and reminding him to avoid accepting requests from others.

In an organizational setting, a precommitment can involve committing to a certain decision or plan publicly. How many times have you seen subversive efforts to undermine plans or decisions by people who disagree with them? Frequently, such behaviors result from the lack of a transparent and thorough decision-making process in which everyone had a chance to buy into the final outcome and make a clear commitment. Instead, what I often see when I am brought in to help address an increasingly toxic culture are decisions and plans made by a small clique who have the political weight of power in an organization. These plans and decisions are often undermined by those who are not part of the clique and did not participate fully in the decision-making process.

When decisions and plans involve significant risk, uncertainty, and disagreements, it can help to make a precommitment to a certain point, called a *Schelling point* by scholars, at which to revisit the agreement. That way, everyone can work together and pull in the same direction until the Schelling point is reached. For instance, an organization I worked with set a Schelling point for the launch of a new product of $14 million in sales in the first six months as the test of whether the launch plan for the new product should be reconsidered; another set a Schelling point of twelve months before evaluating the quality of a new performance evaluation process. In both cases, these precommitments protected team members from the acrimonious debate of whether the product or performance evaluation process is working, as they knew there would either be a potential trigger ($14 million) or definitive date (twelve months) at which to reconsider the decision.

The strategies outlined here stem from extensive research on debiasing and have proven highly effective for readers of my articles and books, for audience members of my speeches, for the many people I've coached, and for employees in organizations for which I consulted. In the following pages, you will learn about their stories, along with specific cognitive biases and the concrete tactics you can deploy to address these faulty mental patterns by retraining your mind to be aligned with your business needs in the modern world.

EXERCISE

I promised exercises, and I always keep my promises. For those who are tempted to skip the exercises and come back to them later, please don't. You're shooting yourself in the foot if you don't do these exercises as you go along with the text of the book. I can cite extensive research that proves you won't get even a third of the benefit of this book if you don't do the exercises, but do you really want me to waste the ink to do so? You haven't put this book down yet, so go a bit further and get your journal out. Get ready to go! Take a few minutes to reflect on the following questions and write down your answers in your professional journal:

   📝 How can you implement the technique of *identifying the various dangerous judgment errors that we are facing and making a plan to address them* in your professional activities? How can you help others in your organization and professional network to do so? What challenges do you anticipate in implementing this strategy and helping others do so, and how will you overcome these challenges?

☑ How can you implement *delaying decision-making* in your professional activities? How can you help others in your organization and professional network to do so? What challenges do you anticipate in implementing this strategy and helping others do so, and how will you overcome these challenges?

☑ How can you implement *mindfulness meditation* in your professional activities? How can you help others in your organization and professional network to do so? What challenges do you anticipate in implementing this strategy and helping others do so, and how will you overcome these challenges?

☑ How can you implement *probabilistic thinking* in your professional activities? How can you help others in your organization and professional network to do so? What challenges do you anticipate in implementing this strategy and helping others do so, and how will you overcome these challenges?

☑ How can you implement *making predictions about the future* in your professional activities? How can you help others in your organization and professional network to do so? What challenges do you anticipate in implementing this strategy and helping others do so, and how will you overcome these challenges?

☑ How can you implement *considering alternative explanations and options* in your professional activities? How can you help others in your organization and professional network to do so? What challenges do you anticipate in implementing this strategy and helping others do so, and how will you overcome these challenges?

☑ How can you implement *considering past experiences* in your professional activities? How can you help others in your organization and professional network to do so? What challenges do you anticipate in implementing this strategy and helping others do so, and how will you overcome these challenges?

✐ How can you implement ***considering the long-term future and repeating scenarios*** in your professional activities? How can you help others in your organization and professional network to do so? What challenges do you anticipate in implementing this strategy and helping others do so, and how will you overcome these challenges?

✐ How can you implement ***considering other people's perspectives*** in your professional activities? How can you help others in your organization and professional network to do so? What challenges do you anticipate in implementing this strategy and helping others do so, and how will you overcome these challenges?

✐ How can you implement ***using an outside view to get an external perspective*** in your professional activities? How can you help others in your organization and professional network to do so? What challenges do you anticipate in implementing this strategy and helping others do so, and how will you overcome these challenges?

✐ How can you implement ***setting a policy to guide your future self and organization*** in your professional activities? How can you help others in your organization and professional network to do so? What challenges do you anticipate in implementing this strategy and helping others do so, and how will you overcome these challenges?

✐ How can you implement ***making a precommitment*** in your professional activities? How can you help others in your organization and professional network to do so? What challenges do you anticipate in implementing this strategy and helping others do so, and how will you overcome these challenges?

CHAPTER SUMMARY

➮ Our mind is defined by the combination of the instinctive and emotional autopilot system, and the deliberate and rational intentional system.

➮ Too many leaders rely excessively on the gut reactions of their autopilot system instead of avoiding comfortable but disastrous courses of action by putting in the often uncomfortable effort of using their intentional system to make wise decisions.

➮ We make a series of systematic and predictable dangerous judgment errors—cognitive biases—because of how our brain is wired, due to a combination of our evolutionary heritage and inherent limitations in our mental processing capacities.

➮ We can train our intentional system to spot and address our systematic and predictable dangerous judgment errors in business and other life areas.

➮ Researchers have found and pioneering business leaders are using a series of techniques to minimize and even completely eliminate cognitive biases in themselves, their teams, and their organizations.

Chapter 2

Who Wants to Be a Loser?

Chapter Key Benefits

✿ Uncover how our intuition and natural tendency to avoid losses counterintuitively results in much greater losses for ourselves and our businesses.

✿ Recognize the systemic and predictable dangerous judgment errors that result from our gut reaction to defend ourselves from losses.

✿ Protect yourself from the often-disastrous consequences of these judgment errors through gaining specific techniques to solve loss aversion.

Patricia certainly didn't want to be a loser. She's a top-notch CPA and worked long hours in her big accounting firm. She received frequent praise from her boss for the quality of her work, including excellent performance reviews. Her coworkers came to her when they had questions and needed insights on challenging issues, loving her willingness to help out.

Yet she kept getting passed over for promotion, year after year, despite making requests and networking with higher-ups. She'd already learned everything there was to learn in her current position and was just going through the motions. She thought about looking for a new job for a couple of years and knew in her heart that a serious job search was long overdue. Unfortunately, she hadn't been able to do it and she didn't know why.

Patricia's dilemma reflects a typical problematic gut reaction that undermines the success of many professionals, including business leaders. However, before talking about this dilemma, let's talk about luck.

Do You Feel Lucky?

It's your lucky day! You meet a kind stranger who offers you a great deal, something for nothing. No tricks! You're getting a free lunch. She offers you a choice: A) She'll give you $45; B) She'll give you a chance to flip a quarter from your pocket. If it's heads, then she'll give you $100. If it's tails, you get nothing.

Which do you choose? Do you want $45 in cold, hard cash, or are you willing to take a chance with the coin flip? Decide before reading further. Keep your choice firmly in your mind.

The next day you have some bad luck. You are stopped by a police officer for going just over the speed limit. He's bored and wants to entertain himself, so he offers you a choice: A) He'll fine you $45; B) He'll give you a chance to flip a quarter from your wallet. If it's heads, he'll fine you $100. If it's tails, he'll let it slide.

Now which of these do you want? Again, make a choice, and keep it firmly in mind. Do you want to try to avoid any losses with the coin flip or hand over your $45?

When I present this scenario in my speeches to business audiences, about 80 percent say they'll take the $45 from the kind stranger, and about 75 percent want to flip a coin to see if the cop will let it slide. So if you made either or both of these choices, you're in good company.

Upon first learning about this scenario from the professor who mentored me in graduate school, I made the same choices. Indeed, the $45 offered by the kind stranger is a sure thing, and it felt good to have the money in my pocket. Wouldn't I feel foolish if I let this certain thing go for just a chance at getting the $100?

By the same token, in the second scenario, I didn't want to lose the money. If I gave the cop $45, that would be a sure loss. If I took the chance at a coin flip, I might not have to pay anything.

So in both cases—the gift and the fine—my gut reaction was to avoid losing out. After all, who wants to be a loser?

My mentor told me that studies on this topic showed that most people made the same choice that I did. Then, he told me to take out a quarter and flip it.

I got heads, so I would have gotten $100, losing out on my choice. Then, he asked me what would happen if I flipped it 10 times, 100 times, 1,000 times, 10,000 times, then 100,000 times. At 100,000, he told me, on average I would get $5 million if I chose the coin flip for $100 each time, versus $4.5 million if I chose $45. The difference: a cool $500,000.

Thus, choosing $45 as my gift and the coin flip as my fine resulted in losing out in both cases. The right choice—the one most likely to not make me a loser—is to choose the coin flip as the gift and the $45 as the fine. Otherwise, over multiple coin flips, I'm very likely to lose.

I was surprised, confused, and hard-pressed to believe him, or at least my autopilot system felt that way. He convinced me by running the numbers. Let's go with the gift first. You're flipping a coin from your own pocket, so you know it's fair. The chance of getting heads is 50 percent, so in half of all cases you'll win $100, and in the rest you won't win anything. That's equivalent to $50 on average, versus $45.

The fine has the same math. By choosing the coin flip, I was giving up $50 on average versus $45.

But wait, Prof. You presented this as a one-time deal, not a repeating opportunity. Maybe if you told me it was a repeating scenario, I'd have thought about it differently.

That didn't fly. He told me that research shows our gut treats each individual scenario we see as a one-off. In reality, we face a multitude of such choices daily in our professional lives. Our intuition is to treat each one as a separate situation. Yet, they form part of a broader repeating pattern where our intuition tends to steer us toward losing money.

Then, he told me something I would never forget: my life—anyone's life—is made of 100,000 coin flips. If we are trying to seize an opportunity, we can either win $5 million or $4.5 million. If we are trying to avoid a threat, we can lose either $4.5 million or $5 million. To avoid having our gut lead us into gaining $500,000 from opportunities and not losing $500,000 from threats throughout the course of our lives—a nice $1 million in total profit—we need to decide right now to see all risks as broad repeating patterns and treat them accordingly.

His words changed my life, and so many things fell into place. I began to see patterns of risk and reward in all repeating situations in my life, both professional and personal. It proved a monumental and very lucrative change in my feeling and thinking patterns.

How can you apply this paradigm shift to yourself? Think about your business. Every day, you face a series of situations for which you need to decide whether to take the course that feels most comfortable by avoiding losses, or the course that feels less comfortable and leads to more gains over time. We're not talking about huge bet-the-company risks, which require a different approach, but the kind of small decisions that add up to large sums over time. If you just go with your gut instead of doing the calculations and going with the data, you are likely to lose much more money by not taking the course that feels most risky.

Now, the difference between $45 and $50 might not seem like much. However, repeated multiple times a day, it means a lot. The difference between these two numbers is 10 percent. If every time you face a business decision—whether addressing threats (fines) or seizing opportunities (gifts)—you take the choice that feels most comfortable to your gut by avoiding losses, the annual cost is 10 percent of your revenue.

Let's say you have a personal income of $100,000 per year. After paying expenses, you save $20,000 a year. That's your profit. If you lose 10 percent of your revenue, or $10,000, you only have $10,000 profit a year. In other words, 50 percent of your profit is wiped out by trying to avoid losses.

Now, reflect on your earlier choices. Did you choose the $45 gift and the coin flip as the fine? In that case, you are vulnerable to both aspects of this problematic gut reaction. Maybe you selected the coin flip as the gift, and the same for the fine? In that case, you are probably more vulnerable to loss aversion when you address threats rather than when you face unexpected opportunities, and will be most vulnerable when unexpected problems arise. How about if you chose $45 for both the fine and the gift? Then you're most likely to be hurt by loss aversion when things are going well and will fail to seize unexpected opportunities, going for the option that feels safest rather than the one that will most help your bottom line.

Perhaps you chose the coin flip as the gift and the $45 as the fine, and are in the minority who focus on making the most profitable decisions. Well, kudos to you!

How about other employees in your organization? Let's say your company has an annual revenue of $50 million, and a healthy profit of $7.5 million. Regardless of the choice you're making, if other employees in your organization are going with their gut to avoid losses, and the company loses 10 percent of its revenue or $5 million per year, then two-thirds of your profit will be wiped out, leaving only $2.5 million.

Incidentally, while 80 percent of all business audiences in my speeches prefer $45 as the gift and 75 percent the coin flip as the fine, the numbers are different when I present to top executives: it's closer to 50 percent for both. Executives are more used to checking their intuitions against profit and loss statements and making decisions that are most profitable. Still, the fact that 50 percent chose to lose 10 percent of their revenue in each case highlights the grave danger of our tendency to avoid losses.

Loss Aversion

The cognitive bias behind our faulty decision-making is called **loss aversion**, our tendency to prefer avoiding losses over getting higher gains. While I used 10 percent as my example, the original research on loss aversion by Amos Tversky and Daniel Kahneman suggests that for many people, the tendency to avoid losses may be twice as strong as their desire for gains.[1]

What explains loss aversion? Let's consider the evolutionary context of the savanna environment in comparison to today's world.

Back then, we had no way of saving resources for the future. If you killed an animal too large for your tribe to eat before it rotted, you couldn't use the remaining meat. If you made too many tools, you couldn't carry them with you when your tribe migrated in search of better hunting grounds. By contrast, if you took risks that caused you to lose the few resources you had, you might easily die in the dangerous savanna environment.

It's no wonder that our ancestors developed an intuitive aversion to losing resources, compared to gaining them. Our gut reactions retain this reluctance in our modern environment, in spite of the much lower danger associated with losing resources now. It's unlikely we will die if we take reasonable risks. Moreover, the banking system and property law enable us to accumulate resources, and the stability of modern life enables us to be relatively secure in this resource accumulation.

Going against your gut intuitions on loss aversion will be worth hundreds of thousands to you personally and many millions to your business throughout the course of your career. What would you pay to get 10 percent higher revenue that adds to your profit margins without any associated costs? It might take much less than you think: simply a slight adjustment in your decision-making strategy.

EXERCISE

Not doing the exercises in this chapter will inhibit your ability to apply these strategies in your professional life. Take the time to reflect on the following questions for a few minutes and write down your answers in your professional journal:

✎ Where have you fallen for *loss aversion* in your professional activities and how has doing so harmed you? Where have you seen other people in your organization and professional network fall for this bias in their professional activities, and how has doing so harmed them?

Pragmatic Dangers of Loss Aversion

How does loss aversion play out in real life? Let's go back to Patricia, the CPA who had difficulty deciding to leave her job. She came to me for coaching on making this decision after being one of the 80 percent at my speeches who indicated she would rather keep the $45 than take the mathematically most profitable option of the coin flip.

She's an accountant and the math proved very convincing for her. What she found more difficult was deciding how to deal with the contradictory impulses she experienced between her gut and her head. After all, having your intentional system know about the problem of loss aversion doesn't mean that it's magically fixed, because the autopilot system still makes avoiding losses the most comfortable option.

In Patricia's case, loss aversion led her to overvalue her current situation and feel reluctant to change it in the face of the uncertainty of a job search, even if she knew intellectually that she was highly qualified and would very likely find a much better job. This excessive orientation toward stability over change is a cognitive bias related to loss aversion called *status quo bias.*[2]

Any leader who tried to launch a change effort is familiar with stubborn resistance from staff who fear any change, even when it is desperately needed. Status quo bias and loss aversion combine to undercut many change efforts. Leading and managing change requires a complex approach that draws on the strategies in the second half of this book.

Status quo bias often comes along with a tendency to try to find excessive information before making decisions. This mental failure mode bears the name ***information bias,*** informally known as "analysis paralysis."[3] You'll often see someone who opposes healthy and needed change demand more and more information, even if that data has no real relevance on the decision at hand.

I've seen the combination of information bias and status quo bias have an especially damaging impact on companies whose growth curve is plateauing. For example, a technology company experienced rapid growth with a couple of innovative products. However, its growth started to decrease following the typical S-curve growth model.

This model accurately predicts the large majority of growth scenarios for successful products, or other successful endeavors. First comes a slow and effortful start-up stage, followed by rapid growth stage. After a while comes a slowdown in growth, often following market saturation or competitive pressure or other factors, where the product reaches maturity. If nothing changes, an inevitable revenue decline follows, due to a combination of external market changes and internal stagnation.

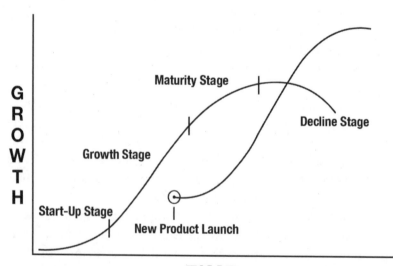

It's common for business leaders to express surprise and confusion over the plateau and decline, despite the typical nature of this growth cycle. The time to change things up and launch new offerings comes during the rapid growth stage, not during the plateau stage. Leaders aware of the S-curve invest into R&D and innovation most when things are going well with established products, to have new products ready to go that would maintain rapid growth.

Unfortunately, the technology company failed to do so. Instead, its leadership focused on analyzing the market to find the cause of the problem when growth began to decrease. There were a couple of executives in the company who proposed launching new products, but most of the leadership was cautious. They kept asking for guarantees and assurances that the products would work out, demanding more information even when additional information wasn't relevant. They instead preferred to double down on the successfully performing products, tinkering with them in hopes of reviving growth.

EXERCISE

Take the time to reflect on the following questions for a few minutes and write down your answers in your professional journal:

📝 Where have you fallen for *status quo bias* in your professional activities, and how has doing so harmed you? Where have you seen other people in your organization and professional network fall for this bias in their professional activities, and how has doing so harmed them?

📝 Where have you fallen for *information bias* in your professional activities, and how has doing so harmed you? Where have you seen other people in your organization and professional network fall for this bias in their professional activities, and how has doing so harmed them?

You Sank My Battleship!

Another typical business example of loss aversion causes many problems for small business owners. How often have you walked into a small business and felt surprised at the dinky furnishings? Many small business owners try to avoid losses by getting cheap décor, yet this strategy ends up costing them more in the long run.

First, low-quality furniture wears out more quickly and has to be replaced more often. Second, and perhaps more importantly, I'm sure I'm not the only one who chose not to work with a small business that conveyed a penny-pinching appearance. After all, if they penny-pinch on their daily surroundings, how do they treat clients?

Unfortunately, the owners of small businesses that are growing into midsize businesses—a group that form a substantial portion of my coaching clients—often feel reluctant to dispose of such furnishings. They suffer from a cognitive bias related to loss aversion called *sunk costs,* which means once we invest significant resources into initiatives and relationships, we tend to hold on to them far longer than we should, even when they no longer provide an acceptable return on investment.[4] It takes a lot of effort to convince them that the money they invested in the décor is gone and they need to focus on projecting a classy appearance to their future customers.

Our propensity to pay excessive amounts to avoid a loss is exemplified by a problematic tendency that I've seen in both small and large businesses: extended warranties. Studies find that such warranties are usually not worth it and are a major profit leader for equipment manufacturers. As long as you have sufficient money to replace the piece of equipment, avoid getting extended warranties.

In general, insurance is structured so that the insurer wins and you lose. Thus, the only insurance that makes sense is coverage for significant problems that you can't easily address through your existing cash flow. Fire insurance makes a great deal of sense; smartphone insurance does not. We tend to place excessive value on products we own, a cognitive bias called the *endowment effect,* which makes it easy for those who understand this quirk of our psychology to take advantage of us.[5]

EXERCISE

Take the time to reflect on the following questions for a few minutes and write down your answers in your professional journal:

📝 Where have you fallen for *sunk costs* in your professional activities, and how has doing so harmed you? Where have you seen other people in your organization and professional network fall for this bias in their professional activities, and how has doing so harmed them?

📝 Where have you fallen for *endowment effect* in your professional activities, and how has doing so harmed you? Where have you seen other people in your organization and professional network fall for this bias in their professional activities, and how has doing so harmed them?

My Baby Is the Most Beautiful Baby

Finally, let's consider a consulting client of mine, a B2B software company that needed my help to improve employee engagement and motivation in selling the company's services. At the tail end of my engagement, the company experienced a serious challenge when a larger company entered the market with a product that competed against one of my client's three flagship products. My client had a relatively small full-time sales force, which made it hard to protect client relationships.

The sales force spread itself thin trying to convince all existing customer accounts to stay with them and avoid switching to the competitor's product. After considering the previous scenario in which the cop levied the fine, this behavior was a mistake. They didn't want to lose any accounts, but of course they would inevitably lose some; the competitor wasn't stupid and was going to gain at least some market share. They suffered from a form of loss aversion known as the *IKEA effect,* where we tend to value too much what we ourselves create in comparison to how much it's actually worth on the open market. In this case, they overvalued the customer relationships they built. The opposite bias happens as well, called *not invented here,* where organizations, teams, and individuals place a too-low value on ideas, products, and techniques found elsewhere.[6]

In the previous example, it would have been much wiser for the sales force to triage aggressively and focus on cultivating the few most important accounts from which the company made most of its money. About twelve accounts out of forty-nine made up more than 70 percent of the company's money, a reminder of the general validity of the Pareto principle (most of the value comes from relatively few sources).

I encouraged the company's VP of sales to change his strategy. I asked him to agree to the loss of many smaller and less important accounts (giving up the $45) in exchange for protecting himself from a much bigger loss (a coin flip for $100, although the company's chances of keeping all the accounts were much lower than a coin flip). We worked together to create a plan where the sales team focused on cultivating the twelve accounts through relationship building and improved customer service, while highlighting the risks of switching to the unproven product offered by the competitor. In the end, the B2B firm managed to keep all twelve large accounts, and more than half of the smaller ones that preferred to stick with the proven product despite the cheaper introductory price offered by the competitor, especially because the bigger accounts did so.

EXERCISE

Take the time to reflect on the following questions for a few minutes and write down your answers in your professional journal:

- ✎ Where have you fallen for *IKEA effect* in your professional activities, and how has doing so harmed you? Where have you seen other people in your organization and professional network fall for this bias in their professional activities, and how has doing so harmed them?

- ✎ Where have you fallen for *not invented here* in your professional activities, and how has doing so harmed you? Where have you seen other people in your organization and professional network fall for this bias in their professional activities, and how has doing so harmed them?

Solving Loss Aversion & Co.

Mindfulness meditation is an excellent practice that will build up your debiasing ability overall, and applies to all judgment errors rather than any one in particular. Thus, I will only discuss it as a solution in this chapter so I don't have to repeat it every time, but keep in mind that it applies to all of the cognitive biases described throughout the book. Note that I focus only on research-backed meditation practices; other approaches exist, and they may be effective, but they haven't been studied enough by academic research for me to be comfortable putting them forward.[7]

A daily sitting practice of just ten minutes a day will substantially improve your ability to solve all sorts of cognitive biases. Due to the general applicability of mindfulness meditation for debiasing, along with other mental and physical well-being benefits, I cannot stress enough the importance of taking up a daily meditation practice.

For those not familiar with meditation, a breathing practice offers a good place to start. Free up thirty minutes for your first meditation session. For future sessions, ten to twenty minutes should be sufficient. Start by sitting in a comfortable position. Then, take in a long breath, counting to five slowly as you breathe in. Hold in your breath for the same five-count length, then breathe out while counting to five. Then, wait for another count of five before breathing in again.

Repeat this cycle a couple more times until you grow comfortable with it. Then, at the start of the next cycle when doing the five-count breathing in, focus on the sensations in your nostrils when the air moves past them. Focus fully on that sensation while still maintaining the pace of slow breathing in. Once you breathe in, keep focusing on your nostrils for the five-count while holding your breath, and notice how they feel different with no air rushing past them. Then, focus once again on air rushing past your nostrils when you breathe out to the count of five, and then once again on the nostrils with no air moving past them while you wait for a five-count before breathing in. Keep doing the five-count breath cycle combined with focusing on your nostrils for twenty minutes. Notice whenever your attention wanders away from your nostrils, and bring it back.

That's not too hard, right? To build up this practice, first you need to make a personal commitment to free up ten to twenty minutes a day. The twenty minutes will give you flexibility for those inevitable days when some unexpected emergency occurs. Those are the days when we feel least capable of meditating, yet counterintuitively, these are the days when meditation can most help us avoid mistakes and make better decisions.

Then, learn about different approaches to meditation and experiment with the three major ones: focusing on breathing, focusing on letting go of thoughts (zazen), and focusing on body awareness. You can search for this information online or read books about it.

After you choose an approach that works best for you, decide on a specific time and place in which you'll engage in your sitting practice. I do my meditation in the morning, shortly after I start my work tasks, as my first break of the day. What reminders will you use to help you remember to pursue this practice? Write down your commitment in a journal or email to yourself, and share with others in your life about your new mental exercise routine.

Be forgiving of yourself if you slip up, and simply get back on the wagon. New habits are notoriously difficult to build. Remember, this mindfulness practice is one of the best things you can do to improve your overall ability to fight dangerous judgment errors in all of your professional activities.

Let's move on to specific techniques for debiasing the cognitive biases described in this chapter, starting with *delaying decision-making.* This technique offers a critical barrier to avoid the temptation of making a choice that causes us to avoid any and all losses. When making any choice that involves a sure but smaller loss or gain, versus a more risky but larger loss or gain, take a minute to consider your options.

For instance, when shopping for computer equipment, cars, washers, dryers, or anything else for which the sales staff offer you an extended warranty, take a minute to think. Will it really pay off to buy it? Most likely not, according to research by *Consumer Reports* and others.

When trying to retain your customers under attack from an aggressive competitor, don't try to protect all of your accounts. Instead, triage to make sure you're investing your sales resources in the most effective manner. What about when you decide to go to an hour-long networking event? You might meet some valuable contacts (or not), but you will definitely lose the resources invested. Consider the mix of potential contacts at the event and how many you'll meet in an hour, and decide whether the time and money you invest are worth the possible contacts you'll gain.

Now, you might think that while the answer is obvious for extended warranties (my apologies for any readers who sell extended warranties, but you know it's one of your biggest profit leaders), the answers are less clear regarding whether to go to the networking event or which accounts to protect from competitors (although you shouldn't try to protect them all). That's fair: it's much easier to address loss aversion and related thinking errors with solid numbers such as $45 versus 50 percent of $100 than in situations with fuzzy and uncertain outcomes.

For these less certain outcomes, the key tool is the technique of ***probabilistic thinking***. With my B2B client facing an attack on its market share from the aggressive competitor, we turned to this technique to decide which accounts to protect. They already had solid numbers on the costs of recruiting new customers versus retaining current ones (it was about six times cheaper to retain current customers). Then, we estimated how the numbers would change as a result of this market change, while supplementing our guesstimates with hard data as it became available. We calculated that the company could likely protect the twelve most important accounts out of forty-nine by dedicating about 60 percent of its sales resources to these large accounts, but we assigned 85 percent to provide a significant margin of safety.

In the case of the technology company, another aspect of probabilistic thinking really helped—launching experiments and making bets—along with the strategy of ***predicting the future.*** I know about this story because one of the executives who wanted the company to push toward innovative products was a coaching client of mine. He asked for my help in convincing the company to get past information bias and status quo bias.

I suggested that he propose a market research experiment: Would the company's existing customers be more interested in what most of the senior management wanted—a slightly improved version of their current products—or some of the suggested ideas bouncing around in the R&D department? A part of the experiment would involve the leadership team predicting what would be of most interest to customers, and making a bet with the company's financial resources on what customers most wanted.

At first, he ran into resistance. First, revealing the R&D ideas seemed foolish to some other senior executives, as competitors might find out and develop these ideas themselves. He pointed out that these offerings wouldn't get developed anyway if the company didn't invest in them. After all, most of the senior leadership wanted to focus on tinkering with existing products. He also proposed to limit the scope of this market research to the trusted contacts within their clients.

Second, the more conservative senior leaders did not want to make a prediction and bet prior to the results of the market research experiment. Yet getting this commitment was fundamentally important to overcoming information bias. They'd otherwise find more ways to obstruct new products, especially because some of them had fiefdoms to protect that were tied to existing products. Eventually, after a private conversation with the CEO, the senior leadership agreed.

You won't be surprised to learn that the market research showed that customers were quite a bit more interested in the new ideas than a slightly improved old product. The company did make an investment into a couple of the new products. Although two failed to make much of an impact, one of the products went on to have even more success than the products that originally launched the growth of the company.

For the networking event and similar scenarios, combine probabilistic thinking with the technique of *considering your past experiences.* At comparable events in the past, how many long-term connections did you make, and how valuable did these connections prove to be? A good way to assess how many connections you typically make is to use the strategy of betting. Would you bet $100 that you would make two connections at this event? How about three connections? When we force ourselves to stake money on the outcome, our thoughts often become much clearer.

If you have difficulty estimating the value of connections, an easy way to do so is to consider how much money you would accept to give up a particular connection. Thus, if you make an average of two connections at an event, and you would give up each of these connections for $80, then the expected probable value of an average event is $160. Reflect on how much time, energy, and money you would have to expend to attend this event, and ask yourself whether it's more or less than $160.

Some of my coaching clients experience challenges when they think about relationships in numerical and especially financial terms. There's something about our tribal background that causes us to treat relationships as distinct and separate from other forms of resources, such as money, time, and reputation. I find such difficulties especially prevalent with clients from East Asia and Latin America, where there's a higher emphasis on group belonging.

However, to avoid judgment errors and avoid relying on our (thoroughly unreliable) gut reactions regarding relationships, we need to tap our intentional system instead of our autopilot system. Using numbers is the easiest and simplest way to do so. Work on de-anchoring yourself if you experience such difficulties. Recognize that your connections are a resource just like everything else.

It's especially tough to recognize the dangers of loss aversion and the related status quo bias when you face a decision to make a major change with uncertain consequences. As a result, evaluating long-term consequences and repeating scenarios is a critical tool for solving loss aversion. Patricia's career choice is a perfect example.

When I asked her why she was so reluctant to look for a new position, she revealed that money was not the only or even biggest issue facing her. She felt comfortable in her current position; she had a clear and steady routine doing the same things every day.

This is a personality trait common to many CPAs. Changing to a new company involves learning a whole new set of systems, processes, and practices, and becoming socialized into a new set of unwritten social norms and rules. Patricia did not look forward to that. Moreover, she genuinely liked her colleagues; she had a positive and supportive social network in her current position. As an introvert, Patricia was worried about the substantial challenges she would experience trying to fit into a new workplace community.

It was no wonder she felt so reluctant to launch a job search. I asked her to imagine her **long-term future and repeating scenarios,** another very useful debiasing strategy for addressing loss aversion. She had been thinking about a new job for the last couple of years. How would she feel if another couple of years elapsed with no promotion and no job search? Patricia had an immediate and visceral reaction of anger and frustration, and surprised herself with the strength of her emotions. She definitely didn't want to be in this dead-end job for another two years!

Then I asked: What is the likelihood that she would be promoted at her current job in the next two years? "Next to none," she answered. To that I replied, "If that's the case, why not simply launch the job search now, and spare yourself the trouble of waiting a couple more years until your anger and frustration overcome your reluctance to get used to new routines and figure out a way to fit into a new work community?"

With that framing, Patricia's internal resistance to finding a new job melted away. She soon launched a job search. In less than two months, she found a more desirable position.

The last important strategy for addressing this category of cognitive biases involves **setting a policy to guide your future self and organization.** Regarding the coin toss, to prevent your intuition from leading you astray, adopt a policy of letting the data lead you, instead of relying on your intuitions. For each decision you face, envision it as a repeating pattern instead of a one-time decision: run the numbers, account for the role of uncertainty, and take the course most likely to lead to the biggest profit. Treating each choice as part of a broader pattern might feel counterintuitive, uncomfortable, and unsafe. Yet the course that feels safe in terms of avoiding losses is actually much more dangerous for your bottom line.

Say you are reluctant to buy more expensive options that will be better for you in the long run. For example, you a small business owner that springs for nice furniture and decorations rather than getting them from a thrift shop, or you pay a website designer to make your website rather than doing it yourself. If so, you can make a personal commitment to go for a more expensive option as your default strategy, thus you have to prove to yourself that it's worthwhile to go for a cheaper option. This approach might feel uncomfortable, but remember that the literature on de-anchoring—and my extensive consulting and coaching experience—suggests that we all tend to undercorrect for our problematic predispositions. It's much better to try to overshoot than to go for what feels comfortable. The same approach applies to setting organizational priorities.

Loss aversion–related cognitive biases are some of the most dangerous ones around for protecting the bottom line of your business; the strategies in this chapter help protect you against them. The next chapter gets into attribution judgment errors, which pose massive threats to the health of your professional relationships.

EXERCISE

Don't lose the benefits of driving these strategies home and figuring out how and where you can best apply them! To ensure you get this value, take a few minutes to reflect on the following questions, and write down your answers in your professional journal:

- How will you use *delaying decision-making* to fight the biases described in this chapter? How will you help others in your organization and professional network use this strategy? What challenges do you anticipate in implementing this strategy and helping others do so, and what steps will you take to overcome these challenges?

- How will you use *probabilistic thinking* to fight the biases described in this chapter? How will you help others in your organization and professional network use this strategy? What challenges do you anticipate in implementing this strategy and helping others do so, and what steps will you take to overcome these challenges?

- How will you use *making predictions about the future* to fight the biases described in this chapter? How will you help others in your organization and professional network use this strategy?

What challenges do you anticipate in implementing this strategy and helping others do so, and what steps will you take to overcome these challenges?

✐ How will you use ***considering past experiences*** to fight the biases described in this chapter? How will you help others in your organization and professional network use this strategy? What challenges do you anticipate in implementing this strategy and helping others do so, and what steps will you take to overcome these challenges?

✐ How will you use ***considering the long-term future and repeating scenarios*** to fight the biases described in this chapter? How will you help others in your organization and professional network use this strategy? What challenges do you anticipate in implementing this strategy and helping others do so, and what steps will you take to overcome these challenges?

✐ How will you use ***setting a policy for your future self and organization*** to fight the biases described in this chapter? How will you help others in your organization and professional network use this strategy? What challenges do you anticipate in implementing this strategy and helping others do so, and what steps will you take to overcome these challenges?

CHAPTER SUMMARY

➡ Our brain is wired to avoid losses even if we can make larger gains on the whole, a dangerous judgment error called *loss aversion.*

➡ Although loss aversion helped our ancestors survive and reproduce in the savanna environment, it devastates our bottom lines in today's business environment.

➡ A particularly dangerous cognitive bias related to loss aversion is *status quo bias,* our reluctance to undertake necessary changes to adapt to the rapidly shifting business context of tomorrow.

➡ Another threat that relates to loss aversion is the judgment error known as *sunken costs,* when we fail to cut our losses into projects and relationships that no longer provide an adequate return on investment. To address dangerous judgment errors related to loss aversion, you can use debiasing techniques that include:
  » delaying decision-making
  » probabilistic thinking
  » making predictions about the future
  » considering past experiences
  » considering the long-term future and repeating scenarios
  » setting a policy for your future self and organization

Chapter 3

Who's the Bad Guy?

Chapter Key Benefits

✿ Learn to mistrust our intuitive evaluations of others that attribute their problematic behavior to their personality and character, while attributing our faults to the external context.

✿ Prevent incorrect snap judgments that harm our professional relationships with clients, peers, vendors, investors, and other stakeholders.

✿ Put into your leadership toolkit the most important techniques for addressing dangerous judgment errors around attributing fault, blame, and motives.

Imagine you are driving on autopilot, as we all do much of the time. Let's be clear: it's a good idea to let your autopilot system be in the driver's seat when you do tasks that require your full focus and attention. In ordinary driving situations—without inclement weather or start-and-stop traffic—you don't need to use your mental resources by turning on your intentional system for driving.

Now imagine you are driving and the car in front of you unexpectedly cuts you off. You slam on your brakes. Maybe you flash your lights or honk your horn. You feel scared and angry. Your sympathetic nervous system activates, shooting cortisol throughout your body. Your heart beats faster, your palms start to sweat, a wave of heat goes through your body.

What's your gut feeling about the other driver? I know my first thought would be that the driver is rude and obnoxious.

Now imagine a different situation. You're driving on autopilot, minding your own business, and you suddenly realize you need to turn right at the next intersection. You quickly switch lanes and hear someone behind you honking the horn. You now realize that there was someone in your blind spot but you forgot to check it in the rush to switch lanes, so you cut the car off.

Do you think that you are a rude driver? The vast majority of us would not. After all, you did not deliberately cut off the other driver; you just failed to see the car.

Let's imagine another situation: your friend hurt herself and you're rushing her to the emergency room. You're driving aggressively and cutting in front of other cars. Are you a rude driver? You'd probably say you are not; you're merely doing the right thing for this situation.

Misattributing Blame

Why do we give ourselves a pass while assigning an obnoxious status to other people? Why does our gut always make us out to be the good guys, and other people the bad guys? There is clearly a disconnect between our gut reactions and reality. This pattern is not a coincidence. Our immediate gut reaction attributes the behavior of other people to their personality, and not to the situation in which the behavior occurs.

The scientific name for this type of thinking and feeling is the *fundamental attribution error,* also called the *correspondence bias.*[1]

This judgment error results in the following: if we see someone behaving rudely, we immediately and intuitively feel that this person is rude. We don't stop to consider whether an unusual situation may cause the individual to act that way. With the example of the driver, maybe the person who cut you off did not see you. Maybe they were driving their friend to the emergency room. But that's not what our autopilot system tells us.

On the contrary, we attribute our own behavior to the situation instead of our personality. Much of the time we believe that we have valid explanations for our actions.

What explains this fallacious mental pattern? From an evolutionary perspective, in the ancestral savanna, it was valuable for our survival to make quick decisions and to assume the worst, regardless of the accuracy of this assumption. In the modern world, where our survival is not immediately threatened by others and where we have long-term interactions with strangers, such judgments about individuals or groups are dangerous.

Don't believe that such snap judgments can be harmful? It may not seem important whether you think wrongly that other drivers are jerks. Sorry to disappoint you, but this mental pattern poses a grave threat to your business relationships.

What would you think of a potential business colleague if you saw her yelling at someone on her smartphone? You would probably have a negative reaction toward her and may not do business with her as a result. What if you found out she was yelling because her father, who misplaced his hearing aid, was on the other line and she was making plans to come help him look for it?

There can be many innocent explanations for someone yelling on the phone, but we are tempted to assume the worst. In another phone-related example, I was coaching a CEO of a company that had many staff who worked from home. He told me about a recent incident that involved an employee who had a heated Skype discussion with an HR manager over a conflictual issue. The Skype call disconnected and the HR manager told the CEO the employee hung up on her. The CEO fired the employee on the spot.

Later, he learned that the employee thought the HR manager hung up on *her*. The call simply disconnected. Unfortunately, it was too late to rescind the termination, even though the CEO regretted his heated decision. This unfair termination demoralized the rest of the staff, which resulted in a growing disconnect between the CEO and other staff. It eventually led to the CEO leaving the organization.

How about when you see a neighbor leave her trash can on the curb long after a garbage truck came through to pick it up? What do you feel about the neighbor when her garbage can is the only lonely can on the whole block? Is it intuitive to feel that the neighbor is just lazy and doesn't care about the appearance of the neighborhood?

I was that neighbor several years ago when my wife Agnes had a nervous breakdown. In addition to my full-time professor job and civic commitments, I became her part-time caretaker, spending an additional fifteen to twenty hours a week and a great deal of emotional and mental energy on this role. It would be an understatement to say that it was an overwhelming experience. I ended up developing a mental illness myself, an anxiety adjustment disorder, which manifested itself mainly as physical fatigue.

Although I tried to take care of all the house chores, some days I had no energy left to roll the trash back from the curb. Would you judge me as lazy and uncaring? I hope not, yet such snap judgments based on limited experience and heated emotions are incredibly easy to make. Of course, they would then powerfully shape your relationship to me as a neighbor.

EXERCISE

Don't blame me if you fail to get substantial value from the chapter as a result of failing to do the exercises. Let's not have any blame at all; take the time to reflect on the following questions for a few minutes, and write down your answers in your professional journal:

✏️ Where have you fallen for *fundamental attribution error* in your professional activities and how has doing so harmed you? Where have you seen other people in your organization and professional network fall for this bias in their professional activities, and how has doing so harmed them?

Snap Judgments About Groups

Snap judgments that misattribute the reasons for behaviors also apply to our evaluations of broad groups, which is called the **group attribution error**.[2] This error comes in two forms: when we perceive that an individual group member reflects the whole group, or when we perceive that the group's overall characteristics determine the nature of individuals in that group.

In the savanna, it was beneficial to our survival to make snap judgments about the tie-in between group and individual, regardless of the accuracy of such judgments. In fact, such judgments might have been more accurate in the prehistoric period of human evolution than in the modern world, as our ancestors all lived in small tribes.

Members depended on the tribe for their survival and shared many characteristics, above all loyalty to the tribe. In the savanna environment, it was a safe bet that if you observed the behavior of a certain tribe member, her behavior largely reflected the overall perspective of her tribe; in turn, if you knew some details about a specific tribe's characteristics, you could have a relatively confident idea of how a member of that tribe would behave.

That's not the case in the modern world. Our society is incredibly complex and diverse. The kind of group affiliations we have now—ethnicity, gender, sexuality, class, culture, religion, political ideology, profession, geographical location—produce multifaceted identities. It's a very poor bet that someone of the same ethnicity, gender, class, and so on will strongly resemble others with the same affiliation; likewise, it's equally irrational to use group membership to make confident judgments about the qualities of someone who belongs to that group.

Tragically, those old instincts still dominate our judgments in the modern world. Group attribution error is one of the most important factors in stereotyping.

Let's say a small family-owned hardware store hires a Pakistani employee for the first time ever. Now, imagine this Pakistani employee is chronically late, so the owner eventually lets this employee go. What's the likelihood that the owner will hire another Pakistani

employee? Much lower than hiring the first Pakistani! The owner
will now attribute lateness to all Pakistanis as a group, wrongfully
painting a whole ethnic group with a broad brush.

I fall for the group attribution error too. I suffer from occasional
back pain, so I went to a chiropractor many years ago. He cracked
my back, and I left worse off than I came. I tried another chiropractor and had a similar experience. After that, I swore off chiropractors
as useless, went to physical therapy, and used other treatments.

However, my friend's dad is a chiropractor, and she convinced
me to try him out; she promised he doesn't do back cracking. (The
only thing he cracked was jokes.) He was great, with methods that
proved much more effective than any other previous treatment. He
found the specific muscles in my back that were out of whack, re-
lieved them, and prescribed very specific and targeted exercises, unlike the physical therapists who recommended a broad set of general
exercises. Considering the crucial role of physical well-being for our
professional success—when so many of us spend our days hunched
in front of our computers or sitting in meetings—this kind of group
attribution error can be a real pain in the back.

As another example, have you ever gone to a professional association meeting or coaching group in your locale? I often recommend
these to my coaching clients, especially those in executive positions.
It can be lonely at the top, as executives usually can't confide in their
staff. Chambers of commerce are one option, professional associations another. Executive-level peer advisory groups, such as Vistage,
Young Presidents Organization, and Entrepreneurs' Organization,
provide a combination of professional development, coaching, and
mastermind opportunities, and are available in most areas around
the US and in many other countries (disclaimer: I speak often for
such groups).

An executive of a community bank in Cincinnati, Ohio, told me
how he went to a networking event for local bankers several years ago;
he had a negative experience with a couple of people he talked with,
left early, and crossed the organization off his list. Knowing about the
group attribution error, you can recognize the irrational nature of this
behavior. A couple of individual members are hardly representative of
the whole. He gave up potentially valuable relationships by making

this error. I convinced him to try again, and commit to approaching at least ten people. He had a much better experience the second time around, and told me that he gained many useful contacts.

What about the reverse: a belief that an individual member of a group is representative of the whole group? Stereotyping applies here as well.

For instance, too many people still believe the myth about Jewish greediness. Thus, they assume that any individual of Jewish background must be greedy. In reality, the 2017 Giving USA report found that the average Jewish household donates $2,526 to charity yearly, compared to $1,749 for Protestants. This disparity is not simply a result of income difference: among households earning less than $50,000, about 60 percent of Jewish households donated some money to charity as opposed to 46 percent of households that are not Jewish.

Moreover, Jews regularly give to non-Jewish causes. The report showed that 54 percent of Jews were more likely to make a donation to social-service charities than to their religious congregation; the comparative number for those who are not Jewish is 41 percent. Still, the myth about Jewish greed is persistent and powerfully shapes perceptions of Jews, making many business leaders reluctant to work with them. As someone who comes from a mixed religious heritage (my dad is Jewish, and my mom is Christian), this myth really bugs me on a personal level, as I saw my dad held back in his professional career due to unjustified stereotypes about Jews.

The same problem plagues negative assumptions about different departments within companies; a good example is the harmful consequences of teamwork. In business advice literature, teamwork is almost invariably portrayed in a positive light. Indeed, it's very beneficial for all employees to have a strong sense of being on the same team. The danger starts when people perceive those in their department to be on one team, and those in other departments to be on a different and even opposing team. Frequently, such harmful team dynamics start when someone from one department has a bad experience with an employee from another department, then extends their assumptions to all other members of that department.

While consulting for a midsize software company on improving organizational culture, I ran into a typical example of this problem.

The sales and marketing department's employees complained to me that the software engineers did not want to work with them on B2B selling of the company's enterprise software product. Diving deeper, I found out that this assumption stemmed from the sales and marketing staff making general requests and individually approaching only a couple of programmers out of the more than 170 in the company.

We worked to revise both the methods used by marketing and sales people to reach out to the software engineers and also made their approach more systematic. As a result, the marketing and sales department found more than a dozen programmers who were glad to help demonstrate the product to clients. They trained the engineers and saw substantially higher conversion rates from prospect meetings when engineers went along to help out. Such cross-team collaboration helped address the negative teamwork dynamics between these departments.

A final attribution bias, the ***ultimate attribution error,*** combines elements of the fundamental attribution error and the group attribution error.[3] The ultimate attribution error causes us to misattribute problematic group behaviors or traits to the internal characteristics of groups that we don't like as opposed to external circumstances and vice versa for groups we like.

The following is a clear example of ultimate attribution error. When I am hired to speak about diversity, I usually share statistics that show white male managers tend to be promoted at a greater rate, offered higher salaries, included within informal networks, and given access to better mentoring than women or ethnic minorities. A number of white male audience members frequently respond by coming up with explanations that do not involve any possibility of discrimination. As an example, they speak about women who take time off to care for their family or certain ethnic minorities that lack a cultural fit in American companies. I respond by showing studies that control for work experience—meaning time worked and the kind of positions held—finding that women earn less than men anyway. Studies also show other forms of discrimination, even within the white male group: taller white males earned higher salaries, and overweight white males had a lower salary.

After highlighting the discrimination against certain white males, I lead into a broader discussion of implicit bias, meaning unconscious negative associations we have because of our tribal background. These associations cause our autopilot systems to express subtle reluctance to support those we don't perceive as part of our tribe. The crucial thing to highlight is that there is no shame or blame in implicit bias, as it doesn't stem from any fault in the individual. This no-shame approach decreases the fight-flight-freeze defensive response among reluctant audiences in diversity and inclusion talks, and helps them hear and accept the issue.[4]

With these additional statistics and discussion of implicit bias, the issue is generally settled. Still, from their subsequent behavior it's clear that some of these audience members don't immediately internalize this evidence. It's much more comforting for their autopilot system to believe that they got ahead through personal competence rather than any privilege; in turn, they are highly reluctant to focus more efforts and energy on uplifting women and ethnic minorities in managerial positions because of the structural challenges facing these groups. The issue of implicit bias doesn't match their intuitions, and thus they reject this concept, despite extensive and strong evidence for its pervasive role in shaping the workplace. It takes a series of subsequent follow-up policy changes and accountability mechanisms to shift an organization's culture, as a single training is almost never sufficient.

The eagerness to attribute lack of professional success by women and ethnic minorities to their internal traits and behaviors is a classic example of the ultimate attribution error, as well as the lack of willingness to acknowledge implicit bias—and sometimes explicit bias, from what I heard from my coaching clients—from white male managers.

EXERCISE

Take the time to reflect on the following questions for a few minutes, and write down your answers in your professional journal:

- 🖊 Where have you fallen for *group attribution error* in your professional activities, and how has doing so harmed you? Where have you seen other people in your organization and professional network fall for this bias in their professional activities, and how has doing so harmed them?

- 🖊 Where have you fallen for *ultimate attribution error* in your professional activities, and how has doing so harmed you? Where have you seen other people in your organization and professional network fall for this bias in their professional activities, and how has doing so harmed them?

Can You Feel Me?

Misattribution of problematic intentions and motivations to groups, as well as individuals, often stems from a cognitive bias called the *empathy gap*, where we underestimate the strength of emotions in other people who do not belong to our group.[5] While blindingly obvious in cases relevant to diversity, the empathy gap plays a less obvious but powerful role in employee motivation and engagement.

For example, too many employers still assume that financial incentives are the only truly important motivator for employees. In reality, extensive research shows that, for employees who have satisfactory salaries, other motivators are of equal or more importance. These range from personal recognition to a sense of meaning and purpose in the workplace, with individual employee personality differences paramount in determining appropriate motivators.

Case in point: a company that provides a range of B2B software solutions saw its sales numbers and customer satisfaction scores gradually decreasing. It wanted its software engineers to do more both to sell the services of the company and to provide outstanding customer service after the sale. Therefore, the company tried to offer its software engineers more money to do selling and customer support. Internal indicators of computer programmer involvement showed that these financial incentives did not result in substantial improvement for sales and customer service. They also tried to motivate software engineers by talking about how improved performance by programmers in these areas would result in greater profitability and client retention. Doing so failed to move the needle.

The company's leadership accused the engineers of being lazy and incompetent. Unfortunately, that's a typical reaction when other people don't act the way we think they should act. We attribute their behavior to negative personality traits rather than the context, and especially not to our failure to motivate them effectively. We're never at fault. They're the jerks (or lazy, or incompetent).

These mistaken assessments frequently stem from our failure to appreciate the vast differences in personality, opinions, beliefs, preferences, values, and habits between ourselves and others. We overestimate the extent to which other people think and feel the way we do, a cognitive bias called the *false consensus effect.*[6] We observe how others act, imagine why we would act that way if we were in their place, and explain their behaviors accordingly, often in negative ways.

At that point, the company's leadership sought outside help and brought me in to assess the situation. After interviewing and observing the software engineers, it became clear that they were primarily emotionally engaged with writing code and solving technical problems, not sales and customer service. Their already-satisfactory salaries meant that additional financial compensation did not make much of a difference, which aligned with the research on employee motivation.[7] The messages about company needs did not resonate with software engineers either.

When I presented this information to the C-suite, the surprised response from the vice president of sales was, "Software engineers have emotions?"

When he said that, everyone in the room laughed. It was the type of laughter made when someone voices something with which you secretly agreed. It's important to understand that the C-suite did not include people who had a background as software engineers. The CEO was hired six months prior to this incident to turn the company around after declining performance. He replaced most senior executives with his own top team, who did not have much experience in the software consulting business, but had strong sales and marketing backgrounds.

Salespeople tend to be quite extroverted and display emotions easily. By contrast, software engineers generally are introverted and avoid public emotional expression.

This classic case of empathy gap represented group differences not driven by factors such as gender or skin color. White males predominated among both the sales staff and the software engineers. The key issue stemmed from personality differences and role differences in the company, which resulted in bad judgment errors about how to motivate engineers.

EXERCISE

Take the time to reflect on the following questions for a few minutes, and write down your answers in your professional journal:

✐ Where have you fallen for *empathy gap* in your professional activities, and how has doing so harmed you? Where have you seen other people in your organization and professional network fall for this bias in their professional activities, and how has doing so harmed them?

✐ Where have you fallen for *false consensus effect* in your professional activities, and how has doing so harmed you? Where have you seen other people in your organization and professional network fall for this bias in their professional activities, and how has doing so harmed them?

Solving Misattributions

The technique of *delaying judgments* helps greatly in· addressing attribution errors. Snap judgments are notoriously unreliable; unlike our ancestors on the prehistoric savanna, we modern people don't need ·to make such judgments for our survival in the vast majority of cases. So when you perceive that you are formulating a judgment of someone, notice that you're doing it. Shift your thought pattern from a set judgment to curiosity. Rather than saying, "What a jerk!" when someone cuts you off, change your internal monologue to "Is he a jerk, or is it the circumstances?"

The natural next step is **considering alternative explanations and options.** Why is a potential business colleague yelling on the phone? Is she mean or trying to help her partially deaf father hear better? Or perhaps she's justifiably upset because a government bureaucracy keeps redirecting her to various clerks when she just wants to get a permit to allow her business to move forward. Is this unfriendly association member representative of the whole group, or is she an isolated outlier? Is the Pakistani employee's lateness characteristic of all Pakistanis or simply this one individual?

Considering other people's points of view is another useful technique. What would it be like to walk in the shoes of someone from another department within your organization? What are their incentives, their perspectives, their beliefs, their needs and wants, and how can you frame your request to achieve your goals? Is it possible that there are substantial differences between people in that department and you can check with many of them to achieve your goals?

Examining alternatives and reflecting on other people's perspectives proved crucial for addressing the empathy gap in the software consulting company. I clarified to the C-suite that because software engineers generally do not display strong emotions in the workplace, it's natural to ignore their underlying motivations and believe they only follow logical and rational incentives, such as money or organizational well-being. However, forgetting that software engineers are driven primarily by emotional incentives made it difficult for this company to motivate them both to sell their expertise to potential customers and to provide outstanding customer service after the sale.

Examining emotional motivations in interviews and focus groups with software engineers, I and other Disaster Avoidance Experts staff found two promising emotional drivers: 1) desire for positive personal reputation outside the company, and 2) social status as a result of peer recognition from fellow software engineers within the company.

To address the motive of personal reputation in the industry, the company changed its messaging to software engineers about the goal of selling their services. It stopped focusing on additional revenue for the company. Instead, the company's communication emphasized how individual software engineers would obtain a higher reputation and gain the status of thought leaders through writing expert blogs and presenting at industry conferences, which was the main way that the company wanted software engineers to sell their services.

The company also provided software engineers with paid time for doing these activities and covered their travel costs. Note that the financial motivation here did not offer a reward for doing these activities, but simply removed costs of time and money as an obstacle.

To address the desire for social status from peers within the company, we took several steps. First, internal communications such as the weekly company newsletter began to highlight programmers who excelled in customer service as rated by customers. It also praised those who marketed their services well via hits on their blogs and presentations at industry conferences. The company also changed the "employees of the month" awards to highlight these accomplishments, as opposed to solving complicated technical challenges. These short-term, easier changes were accompanied by more fundamental, deeper ones, such as transforming the promotion process to put more weight on customer service and marketing excellence. This change tapped into status as much as money, and helped motivate programmers well.

Another strategy to fight attribution mistakes is through an **external perspective on the situation,** especially from someone with expertise on the topic. If the CEO I coached had come to me for advice before firing the employee, I'd have strongly suggested talking to the employee first before taking any drastic action. In turn, my friend's external perspective on my negative experience with chiropractors really helped address my back pain. And hey, to be fair to chiropractors, two negative experiences are a small sample size to make an evaluation on a whole profession.

Sample size is only one component of the broader solution of **probabilistic thinking.** Avoid being too confident about your estimates of reality based on a small sample size! Say you approach another member of a coaching group association and he turns out to be friendly; it's a good time to update your beliefs and average out your experiences. Whenever you can gain more evidence in a cheap manner, make sure to do so. Although it can be costly in terms of money and resources to hire another Pakistani and evaluate her time management skills, you may want to research the subject of time management and Pakistanis online. Believe me, if this was a problem, there would be significant commentary on the Internet, as there is on the loose sense of time by professionals in the Middle East, something I should have researched before agreeing to a consulting contract there. I would have saved myself unneeded aggravation if I had more appropriate expectations going into the situation.

The *base rate probability*, the statistical term for your preexisting knowledge about any given topic, can also help in debiasing the fundamental, group, and ultimate attribution errors. Say you are considering two candidates for promotion—one white male and one white female—whose work experiences make you believe they would be equally effective in the new position. Independent of any other knowledge, it's hard to form a conclusion about which of these candidates to promote. However, having read this chapter, you know that women tend to be promoted at a lower rate than men and have lower salaries.

Thus, with everything else equal on paper, consider the benefits for your bottom line of hiring people who don't fit the traditional white, tall, fit male background. They likely had to work harder to get to the same equal playing field and will prove more productive and create the most profit for you. And I'm telling you that as a tall, non-obese white male.

Behavioral economics research supports this conclusion. A survey of companies that used the 1996 to 1997 National Organizations Survey found that greater ethnic diversity correlates to more customers, higher market share, increased sales revenue, and increased profit overall.[8] Substantial gender diversity is associated with more customers, greater sales revenue, and higher profits. Another study showed that when women occupy at least 30 percent of a company's board of directors positions it correlates with increased profit.[9]

The final debiasing strategy most applicable to these problems is **making predictions about the future.** Predict whether the person who cut you off will cut off other people too. If you observe such behavior, this evidence increases the likelihood that the person is a jerk, although you should still consider the possibility that he is driving his pregnant wife to the hospital. Does the business colleague constantly yell at people on the phone? What about members of an association or coaching group, or employees in a different department? The combination of probabilistic thinking and predictions will help you calibrate your perception of reality.

Using these strategies to address the dangerous judgment errors in this chapter will help you defend your professional relationships. The next chapter will empower you and others in your organization and professional network to see reality clearly, which is critical to avoid disasters and make the best decisions.

EXERCISE

Don't harm your business relationships by failing to do this final set of exercises about how to integrate the strategies on solving these biases into your professional activities, organization, and professional network as well! Take a few minutes to reflect on the following questions, and write down your answers in your professional journal:

📝 How will you use ***delaying decision-making*** to fight the biases described in this chapter? How will you help others in your organization and professional network use this strategy? What challenges do you anticipate in implementing this strategy and helping others do so, and what steps will you take to overcome these challenges?

📝 How will you use ***considering alternative explanations and options*** to fight the biases described in this chapter? How will you help others in your organization and professional network use this strategy? What challenges do you anticipate in implementing this strategy and helping others do so, and what steps will you take to overcome these challenges?

✎ How will you use *considering other people's points of view* to fight the biases described in this chapter? How will you help others in your organization and professional network use this strategy? What challenges do you anticipate in implementing this strategy and helping others do so, and what steps will you take to overcome these challenges?

✎ How will you use *probabilistic thinking* to fight the biases described in this chapter? How will you help others in your organization and professional network use this strategy? What challenges do you anticipate in implementing this strategy and helping others do so, and what steps will you take to overcome these challenges?

✎ How will you use *making predictions about the future* to fight the biases described in this chapter? How will you help others in your organization and professional network use this strategy? What challenges do you anticipate in implementing this strategy and helping others do so, and what steps will you take to overcome these challenges?

✎ How will you use *getting an external perspective* to fight the biases described in this chapter? How will you help others in your organization and professional network use this strategy? What challenges do you anticipate in implementing this strategy and helping others do so, and what steps will you take to overcome these challenges?

CHAPTER SUMMARY

☞ We are most comfortable attributing our own problematic behaviors to the external context of a situation, instead of to our own internal flaws.

☞ By contrast, we usually attribute misbehaviors by others to their character and personality, as opposed to the setting in which they find themselves.

☞ The same mistaken attributions apply to groups: we make too-positive assumptions about groups to which we belong and excessively negative ones about other groups, a problem most obvious in diversity and inclusion, and more subtly damaging elsewhere.

☞ A related dangerous judgment error, the empathy gap, results in us underestimating the strength of emotions in people who do not belong to our group, which undercuts employee motivation and engagement.

☞ To fight misattribution cognitive biases, we can use the following debiasing techniques:
   » delaying decision-making
   » considering alternative explanations and options
   » considering other people's points of view
   » probabilistic thinking
   » predictions about the future
   » getting an external perspective

Chapter 4

What Color Are Your Glasses?

Chapter Key Benefits

✿   Learn about the dangerous judgment errors that result from our gut reaction of seeing the world through filters that match our beliefs, as opposed to seeing reality clearly.

✿   Understand the business risks for ourselves and our organizations failing to overcome our predilection to fall for the comfort of seeing the world through rose-colored glasses.

✿   Secure for yourself and your team the most effective tools to overcome the dangerous judgment errors resulting from failing to perceive uncomfortable truths.

I was struck by a sentence buried deep in a 2018 *Reuters* article about the bankruptcy of the number two US nursing home chain, HCR ManorCare, that accrued more than $7 billion of debt. ManorCare, based in Toledo, Ohio, transferred ownership of its assets, valued at $4.3 billion, to its landlord, Quality Care Properties, with which it signed a master lease for 289 facilities in 2011.

Here's the sentence that struck me (see if you can spot what made me do a double-take): "ManorCare said revenues have failed to cover monthly rent obligations since 2012, a year after the master lease was signed."[1] That's right, only a year after the lease was signed, ManorCare couldn't make its rent.

It kept sliding deeper into debt for the next five years until it declared bankruptcy. ManorCare blamed a range of problems, such as decreased government reimbursement rates, low occupancy in its nursing homes, and a shift to alternative nursing care services such as home health care and retirement communities.

The question that popped into my head was: Why didn't Manor-Care's executive team foresee these problems down the road? They didn't know that the government reimbursement rates would decrease? Didn't they have statistics on the occupancy in their nursing homes? Wasn't the shift to home health care and retirement communities obvious as well?

I was paying particular attention to ManorCare because I had a speech lined up later that year at the Ohio Health Care Association. As I do for all of my speeches, I read up on the region's industry to customize my content and make it highly relevant to the audience. After my presentation, I talked with a number of long-term health care executives about the ManorCare fiasco. They all told me that the trends on which ManorCare blamed its problems were clearly visible long before 2011, the year it signed the contract that doomed it.

Perhaps you are wondering if ManorCare had new leadership, and because of that change, they couldn't have predicted this problem? Nope. CEO Paul Ormond was at the company's helm for thirty-two years before he left (or was forced out of) his position in September 2017. It was under his leadership that ManorCare became one of the two largest nursing home operators in the nation.

Incidentally, he got a payment of more than $116 million as part of the bankruptcy proceedings.

So how could this long-time executive and his well-experienced team drive a billion-dollar giant over a clearly visible fiscal cliff? More importantly, if it happened to them, could it happen to you?

Seeing Is Believing? Not Really!

Research shows it can happen to all of us—yes, including you and me. No one is immune. If you think you might be, go back and re-read the first chapter about gut reactions.

Remember what I mentioned in an earlier chapter about the four-year study by *LeadershipIQ.com*, which interviewed 1,087 board members from 286 organizations that forced out their chief executive officers?[2] It found that almost one quarter of CEOs—23 percent—got fired for denying reality. In other words, they refused to recognize clearly visible negative facts about the organization's performance. Plenty of top executives join Paul Ormond in failing to see very obvious and very unpleasant facts about their businesses.

In September 2015, the German car giant Volkswagen acknowledged that it used cheating software in its VW and Audi cars to give false readings when the cars underwent emission tests. Known as Dieselgate, the revelation shook up the car industry and led to the resignation of CEO Martin Winterkorn, along with several other top leaders. VW's stock fell more than 40 percent throughout the next few days, and the overall cost of the scandal to the company has been estimated at more than $20 billion. Of course, the discovery of this falsehood was inevitable, just as Enron, WorldCom, and Tyco's accounting frauds were.

It is mind-boggling that top CEOs can ignore facts, but they are not the only ones guilty of doing so. Indeed, a Harvard Business School professor, Richard Tedlow, wrote a book dedicated to the topic of denial in business settings. He found that such denialism is a fundamental component of many business disasters, calling it the greatest obstacle business leaders face.[3] I wouldn't go as far as he does when he says "greatest obstacle." Still, my experience as a consultant and coach agrees with his and others' research findings: failing to see a business reality that's in front of your nose is a huge problem at all levels in all organizations, as well as for solopreneurs.

Whereas ManorCare, Enron, and Volkswagen are billion-dollar disasters, smaller versions of the same problem occur every day. Why do you think research shows that most restaurants fail in less than three years after opening their doors?[3] It's not like their owners set out to fail. It's simply that they didn't (or didn't want to) see the truth about the marketplace.

After all, staring unpleasant truth in the face challenges our self-identity as successful. Many leaders work very hard to convey an appearance of success to themselves and others, and reject any sign they might have made a mistake. This unwillingness to acknowledge mistakes is one of the worst—and unfortunately all too common— qualities of leaders who are otherwise excellent.

Perhaps you're neither a giant like Volkswagen nor a small business like an independent restaurant, but somewhere in the middle market, with a revenue of $10 million to $1 billion. Nope, still not safe.

As a small example, many midsize businesses lose—sometimes dramatically—when pursuing what they see as winning synergy through mergers and acquisitions. Their leadership doesn't pay attention to extensive research that shows mergers and acquisitions fail to increase value for shareholders between 70 to 90 percent of the time.[5] These failures happened, not in companies run by dummies, but by experienced, smart people who had a great deal of success in the past. If you're pursuing a merger or acquisition, you better be very confident that you are much, much better than the people who ran those companies, and understand thoroughly everything that made their merger or acquisition a failure before you pursue your own. The takeaway from this is that the old phrase "seeing is believing" simply doesn't apply to uncomfortable business realities.

Confirming Our Biases

So what's going on here? Why do so many business leaders who are generally perceived as highly competent and successful wear rose-colored glasses that prevent them from seeing obvious points of failure—everything from minor bumps to fiscal cliffs?

They are brought down by a series of related mental errors, the most prominent and well known of which is ***confirmation bias.***[6] It involves two parts. First, we look only for information that confirms preexisting beliefs, as opposed to disproving them. Second, we actively ignore any information that contradicts these beliefs, rather than putting a high value on this information.

You can hear echoes of the second part of the confirmation bias in Upton Sinclair's famous phrase: "It is difficult to get a man to understand something, when his salary depends on his not understanding it." Paul Ormond still received a nice salary while driving ManorCare deeper into debt between 2011 to 2018, instead of admitting his grave failure of signing a terrible lease and trying hard to change the situation while ManorCare still had the financial resources to do so.[7] According to investigators who charged Martin Winterkorn with fraud and conspiracy in May 2018, the former Volkswagen CEO apparently approved the use of the "defeat device" to falsify emissions standards, despite the obvious fact that eventually word would leak and the company, as well as his personal reputation, would be devastated.[8]

When you look for examples of information that confirms preexisting beliefs, you find leaders of large or midsize businesses who launch mergers and acquisitions, as well as entrepreneurs who start up restaurants, without first examining thoroughly the base rates and typical causes of failure for both types of endeavors. It's very typical for business leaders at all levels to look only for information that justifies their business case. I've sat in on more than a dozen meetings for clients during which senior executives waxed enthusiastically about a proposed acquisition or merger. Yet, not a word was uttered about the all-too-typical failures of such ventures. Fortunately, I was able to provide the needed (even if not very popular) service of throwing some cold water on these hyped-up plans. What about the numerous meetings where I—or someone else who could provide this dose of reality—wasn't present?

It takes a lot of guts for someone from inside an organization to break the atmosphere of "make nice" if the organization doesn't have a culture of healthy disagreement and searching for potential problems. Moreover, besides the confirmation bias, they have to face the related problem of **belief bias**, a mental failure mode where our desire to believe the conclusion warps our evaluation of the evidence.[9] Combined with the confirmation bias, belief bias makes it very hard to oppose strategies when high-level executives explicitly endorse them.

Although theses biases are obviously very dangerous for the health of our bottom lines in the modern context, they helped facilitate our survival in the savanna. Back then, it was much less important for us to figure out what was true than to align our perceptions about reality with those of our tribe. We are the descendants of those early humans who succeeded in doing so. As a result, our gut reaction is to be very uncomfortable when we face information that goes against the beliefs of others in our tribe, especially authority figures such as the CEOs of ManorCare, Volkswagen, or Enron, or a top executive dead set on a foolhardy acquisition.

EXERCISE

I know it can be really uncomfortable to face the cold, hard truth of reality, and I believe in your ability to stretch your comfort zone and avoid the harsh fate of many leaders and professionals who fell into denialism and ruined their careers. You can advance that outcome by doing all the exercises in this chapter. Take the time to reflect on the following questions for a few minutes, and write down your answers in your professional journal:

✎ Where have you fallen for **confirmation bias** in your professional activities, and how has doing so harmed you? Where have you seen other people in your organization and professional network fall for this bias in their professional activities, and how has doing so harmed them?

✍ Where have you fallen for *belief bias* in your professional activities, and how has doing so harmed you? Where have you seen other people in your organization and professional network fall for this bias in their professional activities, and how has doing so harmed them?

Stick My Head Where?

Scholars have a specific term for what happens when we actively deny negative reality that's staring us in the face. You won't be surprised that it's called the *ostrich effect,* a cognitive bias named after the (ironically mythical) notion that ostriches stick their heads in the sand whenever they see a threat.[10]

I fell for it during the economic downturn following the 2008 fiscal crisis, when a number of clients stopped returning my calls. I didn't want to face the negative economic reality and failed to reorient as quickly as I should have in pursuing a more appropriate business strategy. In the midst of recovering from the tough times they faced, clients didn't have the energy or focus to invest in my services, even if that was when they could have used them most to avoid problems down the road. I eventually had to cut expenses much more drastically than would otherwise have been the case, and I still regret making that mistake.

What exacerbated the problem for me in 2008 was the *normalcy bias,* our tendency to underestimate both the probability and the impact of a major disaster.[11] I did not realize the devastating extent of the Great Recession; I believed it would be a much shorter and quicker crisis than it proved to be.

The normalcy bias applies to individual companies and people as well as major global disasters. Consider the 1995 collapse of the Barings Bank in London. Nick Leeson, its head derivatives trader in Singapore, made a series of unauthorized bets on the Japanese markets from 1992 to 1995. He was able to hide more than $1.3 billion (yes, that's a "b," not an "m") in losses, due to what a later investigation called "a failure of management and other internal controls of the most basic kind."[12] The bank went bankrupt, all because its leadership could not imagine—and did not institute appropriate controls on—the kind of disaster that Leeson brought about.

Let's consider another example at a real estate management company for which I consulted. A manager refused to acknowledge that a person hired directly by her was a bad fit, despite everyone else in the department telling me that the employee was holding back the team. The other members dropped hints to the manager but didn't want to bring up this matter directly. She was known to express anger at those who brought her bad news, a cognitive bias known as the **MUM effect,** and more colloquially as **shooting the messenger.**[13] Not a healthy tendency for avoiding confirming our biases, as you can well imagine.

EXERCISE

Take the time to reflect on the following questions for a few minutes, and write down your answers in your professional journal:

- ✐ Where have you fallen for the **ostrich effect** in your professional activities, and how has doing so harmed you? Where have you seen other people in your organization and professional network fall for this bias in their professional activities, and how has doing so harmed them?

- ✐ Where have you fallen for **normalcy bias** in your professional activities, and how has doing so harmed you? Where have you seen other people in your organization and professional network fall for this bias in their professional activities, and how has doing so harmed them?

- ✐ Where have you fallen for the **MUM effect** in your professional activities, and how has doing so harmed you? Where have you seen other people in your organization and professional network fall for this bias in their professional activities, and how has doing so harmed them?

I Can Do Anything Better Than You!

Let's move on to a different failure mode affiliated with confirmation bias, a problem I often see undermining teamwork and collaboration, namely, when people tend to claim credit for success and deflect blame for failure. You might call this human nature, but behavioral science scholars call this the *self-serving bias.*[14]

When I conducted a needs analysis on improving employee engagement and teamwork for a US factory of a large international car manufacturer, I noticed that the teams the organization tried to build experienced substantial internal tensions. The existing culture favored individualism and competition over teamwork and collaboration, an atmosphere in which self-serving bias thrives. We had to address this problem as part of the broader effort to increase teamwork in the factory.

A related problem at a biotechnology company for which I consulted stemmed from the rumor mill, which passed along gossip that included many outright lies. Unfortunately, the more frequently people hear a claim, the more they believe it, regardless of whether it's true, a phenomenon known as the *illusory truth effect.*[15] In other words, hearing the same falsehood over and over again, whether from the same person or not, makes us more likely to believe it's accurate. See what I did there? I had two sentences that meant exactly the same thing, but you believed me more after reading the second sentence. That's a perfect illustration of the illusory truth effect.

This cognitive bias is a specific case of a broader phenomenon known as the *mere exposure effect,* where simply being exposed to some external stimulus reduces the perception of novelty and potential threat, and makes us more comfortable with it.[16] Hearing the same rumor many times makes people more comfortable with the rumor. Our gut reactions mistake the feeling of comfort for the feeling of truth, and employees believe the rumors.

EXERCISE

Take the time to reflect on the following questions for a few minutes and write down your answers in your professional journal:

☑ Where have you fallen for *self-serving bias* in your professional activities, and how has doing so harmed you? Where have you seen other people in your organization and professional network fall for this bias in their professional activities, and how has doing so harmed them?

☑ Where have you fallen for *illusory truth effect* and *mere exposure effect* in your professional activities, and how has doing so harmed you? Where have you seen other people in your organization and professional network fall for this bias in their professional activities, and how has doing so harmed them?

Halos and Horns

Our tribal nature causes us to ignore negative information about people we perceive as part of our tribe, and vice versa for those we don't, which leads to two linked cognitive biases. The **halo effect** describes a mental error we make when we like one important characteristic of a person; we then subconsciously raise our estimates of that person's other characteristics. Conversely, the **horns effect** reflects the mistake of subconsciously lowering our estimates of a person when we don't like one salient characteristic.[17]

These biases usually start with our perception of tribal affiliation, meaning whether that person belongs to a group with which we identify. If you ever walked into an office and were struck by the similarities between the personalities, physical appearance, and background of the staff, then you know what I mean. The halo effect and the horns effect are especially dangerous in promotion and assessment.

They critically undermine diversity and inclusion efforts, which not only lead to calamitous legal action and terrible PR crises, but are simply bad business. Much research suggests that visible diversity—for example racial and gender—improves a company's bottom line. Likewise, invisible diversity such as differences in personality and perspectives facilitates better decisions, which also improve profits.

EXERCISE

Take the time to reflect on the following questions for a few minutes, and write down your answers in your professional journal:

☑ Where have you fallen for the *halo effect* in your professional activities, and how has doing so harmed you? Where have you seen other people in your organization and professional network fall for this bias in their professional activities, and how has doing so harmed them?

☑ Where have you fallen for the *horns effect* in your professional activities, and how has doing so harmed you? Where have you seen other people in your organization and professional network fall for this bias in their professional activities, and how has doing so harmed them?

Taking Off the Rose-Colored Glasses

Taking off the rose-colored glasses of confirmation bias and similar biases is easier said than done! Doing so goes directly against our intuitions, even more so than most other cognitive biases, as it may mean sacrificing our sacred cows. It's especially important to train ourselves to turn on our intentional system and avoid relying on the autopilot system to protect ourselves from confirmation bias.

Fortunately, there's extensive research on debiasing this bias; scholars focus on it because of how dangerous this problem tends to be. The most important strategy with the strongest impact as shown by research involves *considering alternative options and explanations.* For instance, if you hear consistent rumors through the grapevine about proposed layoffs, before polishing your resume, look for disconfirming evidence to fight the illusory truth effect. Is the economic situation in your industry or your company looking up or down? Is your supervisor looking worried or relaxed?

Take a similar approach to shaping the strategy of a company. As I talked several clients out of mergers and acquisitions (M&A) initiatives, and encouraged others to pay a much lower price than they intended, I focused on getting them to consider what would happen if their envisioned synergies didn't materialize and what would happen if they uncovered unexpected problems. After all, investment banks that facilitate mergers and perform "due diligence" are highly incentivized to make a sale to get a high fee. It's essential to have someone who doesn't have a stake in the deal to defend the company's money by arguing thoroughly for the alternative perspective and find evidence that casts doubt on an acquisition. Consider getting a retired company executive, an outside consultant, a member of the board of directors who wasn't involved in the acquisition planning, or someone else who can be maximally impartial.

As an example, one midsize law firm of several hundred lawyers was considering an acquisition of a smaller firm (just under a hundred employees). However, the area of expertise did not line up well with the expertise of the smaller one, and the price was pretty steep because the smaller one had other suitors. Likewise, the initial acquisition conversations showed some clashes between the internal culture at the two firms.

Another thing that helped convince the client to avoid the acquisition was the strategy of **_probabilistic thinking,_** particularly considering the base rates. I showed them—and every other client considering acquisitions and mergers—the astoundingly high failure rate of such endeavors. From a probabilistic perspective, it was even more likely for such failure to occur in cases where the leadership did not have extensive M&A experience. The law firm's leadership did not.

I was hired to argue for the "no" side and encouraged the client to compare the acquisition of this smaller firm to the next best alternatives, which in this case included saving money and time and focusing on their own business, or finding another firm to acquire. Eventually, my client decided to let go of this opportunity and undertake due diligence for future acquisitions that considered more thoroughly both expertise and cultural alignment. They did end up acquiring a smaller firm just over a year later after performing a much more thorough due diligence. The firm was much more aligned both culturally and in expertise, and the merger was quite successful.

We know that we tend to overvalue other people who are like us, and undervalue those who are not—the halo effect and the horns effect. So how do we go against our intuitions and address these problems to hire a diverse work force? That was the question posed to me by the regional manager of a New York City clothing store chain who oversaw about 4,000 staff members. She saw a presentation I did on diversity and inclusion at an HR conference and brought me in to consult on the lack of diversity in the store sales staff, which was causing a problem with selling to the diverse customers who entered the stores. Based on testing, the clothing store chain found that stores with more diverse staff (and everything else being equal) had higher sales volume.

The manager adopted the standard approach of using a structured interview process with points for each question to incentivize diversity hires, along with training in cultural competency to facilitate effective recruiting and interviewing. However, she still did not have nearly as much diversity as she wanted.

After I examined her hiring process, I helped her recognize the problem. The traditional approach to incentivizing diversity hires, while crucial, only helps address the horns effect, the tendency to avoid hiring people who are different. Unfortunately, it does not address the halo effect, the tendency to hire people who are like you.

So we worked to revise the structured hiring process. We specifically focused on the structured interview process, and combined probabilistic thinking and the use of numbers with the strategy of setting a policy to guide the organization. To address the horns effect in a more thorough manner, we had interviewers give interviewees positive points for all characteristics in which the interviewee and interviewer differed. These characteristics included traditional diversity categories but also less visible ones, such as socioeconomic backgrounds, accents, cultural preferences, and so on. In turn, to address the halo effect, we had the interviewer give the interviewee negative points for any characteristics, visible and invisible ones, in which the interviewer and interviewee were similar. We also gave additional positive points for the specific areas of diversity that the manager felt were lacking in each store.

It took some time to change the hiring process. We faced some resistance from the hiring staff at first, especially about giving negative points for similarities. They did not feel it was fair to "punish" job candidates just because they were similar to the interviewer. It took substantial training to get them to see that it's a natural human trait to rate people more highly if they liked one aspect of the person. Eventually, we were able to get the hiring staff on board and implement the new process. As a consequence, the new hires grew much more balanced and resulted in the kind of diversity—and eventually the kind of sales revenue—the regional manager wanted.

The probabilistic thinking base rate approach also applies to opening new restaurants. Prior probability suggests it's a very risky idea, so your restaurant business plan better have some special sauce (insert drum roll here) before you proceed.

Let's say you decide to proceed with your restaurant or merger effort despite the base rate. To help improve your estimates of success, use the probabilistic thinking approach of launching experiments to gain additional valuable information and update your probabilities of success or failure before you go all-in on your bet. Can you rent a food truck to see whether your recipes have sufficient appeal? Can you launch a partnership prior to the merger to see if the envisioned synergies on increased revenue or lowered costs actually exist?

To protect yourself from the ostrich effect, **consider the long-term future and repeating scenarios** and combine that with another strategy, **making predictions about the future,** in the areas of potential threat and revising your predictions regularly. Doing so can tell you whether your current course is serving you well. If I had made predictions during the 2008 fiscal crisis, I would have had a hard time fooling myself about my client base drying up. If ManorCare's leadership had considered the long term, it would have seen that there were no good options if it chose to proceed with the existing lease instead of admitting they goofed when signing it and renegotiating the agreement. If Volkswagen's executives made predictions about future threats, they would have had a hard time approving the cheating device, due to the catastrophic legal and PR threat it entailed.

Fixing the problem of self-serving bias necessitates the strategy of **considering other people's perspectives.** If you were in their shoes, how would you decide who deserves credit and who deserves the blame? It helps to make this explicit by talking about this issue in a team, and putting numbers on credit and blame. It might sound weird at first, and it takes some time to integrate into a team, but it works wonders to address hidden resentments and frustrations. That approach helped improve teamwork and collaboration for the car factory I mentioned earlier.

To address the problem of the MUM effect, it greatly helps for those in leadership roles to use the strategy of *making a precommitment* by very explicitly showing in words and actions that they reward and celebrate those who bring them true but negative information. If you are a leader, make such statements often, and then praise publicly those who bring you such information; integrate doing so into the evaluation process for bonuses, raises, and promotions to show that you're not giving lip service to this notion. If you're not in a leadership role, underline and show this section of the book to your supervisor (or buy him a copy) and talk with him about how much the organization can gain from this practice.

I know what you might think at this point: That's all very nice, and I am totally committed to avoiding the confirmation bias and affiliated cognitive biases. However, how do I address a situation in which a colleague, especially someone above me in the hierarchy, falls into these problematic modes of thinking?

That's one of the most frequent questions I get asked in the Q&A during my presentations when I bring up the problem of confirmation bias and other similar judgment errors. Fortunately, one of my areas of academic research—as well as my consulting and coaching practice—focuses on how to get people to accept uncomfortable facts.

Doing so involves a technique distinct from the ones you use when addressing cognitive biases within your organization, team, or yourself. It requires that you have a great deal of evidence to support your position, as well as some practice in low-risk settings with this technique. Otherwise, you're liable to use it incorrectly and have it backfire. Don't blame me if it happens, so proceed at your own risk.

Remember the manager at the real estate management company who was reluctant to acknowledge she had hired the wrong employee? I was in a somewhat precarious political position with her; although she was the subordinate of the person who hired me, if I pissed her off, she could complain to the big boss who hired me or subtly resist the change efforts I was working on inside the company.

The technique I used with that manager, and in many similar situations, can be summarized under the acronym **EGRIP (emotions, goals, rapport, information, positive reinforcement).** EGRIP offers a highly useful tool to get professional colleagues to change their minds toward the truth.[18]

Rather than offer facts, as most of us are tempted to do, start by figuring out the *emotions* that inhibit your colleague from seeing reality clearly. Use curiosity and subtle questioning to figure out her *goals* so that you understand the kind of underlying framework that results in false beliefs on the part of your colleague. Once you understand your colleague's perceptions of the situation, build up *rapport* by showing you care about her goals and empathizing with her emotions. Doing so cultivates both an intellectual and emotional bond, tapping into the mind and heart alike, and places you within her tribe. Now you can work together to address mutual concerns.

Remember the manager with the problematic employee? I had a conversation with her about the role she saw her current and potential future employees playing in the long-term future of her department. I echoed her anxiety about the company's financial performance and concerns about getting funding for future hires, which gave me an additional clue into why she was protecting the incompetent employee.

After placing yourself on the same side of building trust and establishing an emotional connection, move on to the problem at hand: the employee's emotional block. The key is to show the person without arousing a defensive or aggressive response, how his or her current truth denialism undermines the employee's own goals in the long term. This is the first step where you share uncomfortable *information*—step four, not step one.

I asked the manager to identify which of her employees contributed most to her goals for the department's long-term performance, which contributed the least, and why. It was crucial for me to have the numbers available without revealing that I had this information. I also asked her consider who contributed the most to the team spirit and unit cohesion, and who dragged down morale and performance. Knowing that she valued behavioral economics, I brought up research on why we sometimes make mistakes when we evaluate colleagues and how to avoid them.

After some back and forth, she acknowledged that the employee in question was a poor performer and a drag on the group. Together, we collaborated on a plan of proactive development for the employee; if he did not meet agreed-upon benchmarks, he would be let go.

For colleagues accepting the facts, conclude your conversations with *positive reinforcement* without any hint of condescension, an effective research-based tactic for changing people's behaviors through getting them to feel positive emotions about new behaviors. If the person can associate positive emotions with the ability to accept negative facts as an invaluable skill, the less likely it is that anyone will need to have the same conversation with her in the future. I praised her for the courage it took to make a tough decision about the employee, and she expressed appreciation for my positive words, which she acknowledged she got too seldom in her role.

Does that sound manipulative? Step back and recognize that all of our social interactions with each other are manipulations of some sort or another. Some people are just naturally better at it than others and we call them "leaders with charisma" or "good salespeople." Hundreds of my clients prevented disasters for their organizations' bottom lines by using evidence-based methods like EGRIP, which only works when the person whom you're trying to convince holds false beliefs at odds with their own goals. I welcome you to use it throughout your business career as well. And if you ever see me holding mistaken beliefs, I urge you to use it on me too!

Deploying these strategies will empower you and others around you to avoid business disasters by fixing biases that prevent us from seeing reality clearly. In the next chapter, you'll gain the benefit of knowing when and how to be confident about your judgments.

EXERCISE

To avoid confirming your preexisting beliefs and help others in your organization and professional network do so as well, complete these exercises before going to the next chapter! Take a few minutes to reflect on the following questions, and write down your answers in your professional journal:

✐ How will you use *considering alternative scenarios and options* to fight the biases described in this chapter? How will you help others in your organization and professional network use this strategy? What challenges do you anticipate in implementing this strategy and helping others do so, and what steps will you take to overcome these challenges?

✐ How will you use *probabilistic thinking* to fight the biases described in this chapter? How will you help others in your organization and professional network use this strategy? What challenges do you anticipate in implementing this strategy and helping others do so, and what steps will you take to overcome these challenges?

✐ How will you use *making predictions about the future* to fight the biases described in this chapter? How will you help others in your organization and professional network use this strategy? What challenges do you anticipate in implementing this strategy and helping others do so, and what steps will you take to overcome these challenges?

✐ How will you use *considering the long-term future and repeating scenarios* to fight the biases described in this chapter? How will you help others in your organization and professional network use this strategy? What challenges do you anticipate in implementing this strategy and helping others do so, and what steps will you take to overcome these challenges?

✐ How will you use *considering other people's perspectives* to fight the biases described in this chapter? How will you help others in your organization and professional network use this strategy? What challenges do you anticipate in implementing this strategy and helping others do so, and what steps will you take to overcome these challenges?

☑ How will you use ***making a precommitment*** to fight the biases described in this chapter? How will you help others in your organization and professional network use this strategy? What challenges do you anticipate in implementing this strategy and .helping others do so, and what steps will you take to overcome these challenges?

☑ Finally, how will you use ***EGRIP (emotions, goals, rapport, information, positive reinforcement)*** to help those in your organization and professional network fight these biases? What challenges do you anticipate in implementing this strategy, and what steps will you take to overcome these challenges?

CHAPTER SUMMARY

➽ We usually deny unpleasant business realities when they are uncomfortable to our gut.

➽ Our intuitions push us to look for information in making business decisions that matches our existing beliefs, as opposed to evidence that might go against these beliefs.

➽ We greatly underestimate the possible business impact of major disasters.

➽ Our instinct is to claim credit for ourselves for success and deflect blame for failure.

➽ We fall too easily for repeated rumors in business settings.

➽ When we like one important characteristic of a person, our gut moves us to overestimate all other positive aspects of that person and downplay any negatives; the reverse happens when we don't like one important characteristic.

☛ To address these tendencies to confirm our predispositions and instead see reality clearly to make good decisions, the following techniques are most helpful:

» considering alternative scenarios and options
» probabilistic thinking
» making predictions about the future
» considering the long-term future and repeating scenarios
» considering other people's perspectives
» making a precommitment
» EGRIP (emotions, goals, rapport, information, positive reinforcement)

Chapter 5

Should You Be Confident?

✿ Identify the business situations when confidence is critically important, and when it's very dangerous.

✿ Grasp the financial risk of following typical advice to leaders to go forward confidently through learning the dangerous judgment errors associated with such behavior.

✿ Navigate safely through the hidden rocks of confidence-related errors by gaining the techniques needed for you and your organization to address such mistakes.

What's your favorite ice cream flavor? Chocolate? Cookies and cream? Don't tell me it's vanilla!

My favorite flavor is Bangkok Peanut, which combines peanut butter, coconut, honey, and cayenne pepper. Sound unusual? It's one of many unique flavor combinations offered by Jeni's Splendid Ice Creams, a high-end ice cream company in my hometown of Columbus, Ohio (go Bucks!). I'll go ahead and say that its the best ice cream I've ever had in the more than twenty years of traveling to speak and consult across the United States.

In late April 2015, my wife and I went to Jeni's and were quite surprised to find it closed. When we returned home, I looked up what happened. Turns out that listeria, a type of bacteria that causes serious and sometimes fatal illness, was found in a randomly tested pint of Jeni's ice cream, fortunately before it reached customers.

The company took the ethically responsible step of an immediate voluntary recall. Jeni's destroyed more than half a million pounds of ice cream, at a cost of more than $2.5 million. An investigation traced the source of the problem to a pint-filling machine, and Jeni's budgeted $200,000 into preventing a listeria incident in the future.

After a month, the company reopened its scoop shops. My wife and I gladly went to one; I got Bangkok Peanut and my wife got Brambleberry Crisp.

A happy ending? Not exactly.

Less than a week after we got our ice cream, I saw a headline in my local newspaper that Jeni's found listeria in its factory again, and closed its scoop shops as a result. Fortunately, my wife and I did not get sick, nor did anyone else, but the headline was quite a shock to us.

Jeni's reopened its doors again, but we became more cautious and didn't go there for a while. I did some more research on the situation at Jeni's and was sad to find that in eight visits, Food and Drug Administration (FDA) inspectors found problems with cleanliness and pathogen controls. I'll spare you the unpleasant details, but it was more than enough to make my wife and I avoid Jeni's until they fixed these problems.

Now, the FDA is no hero. Plenty of my clients had unfortunate run-ins with government bureaucracies during which inspectors acted too aggressively and hindered the success of promising businesses.

Still, in the context of previous health and safety concerns, I decided to rely on the external verification of FDA inspectors as to when it would be safe to have Jeni's ice cream again.

I'm glad I put my trust in them. A series of further FDA inspections again discovered listeria in samples collected from Jeni's in January 2016. They also found that while Jeni's fixed many of the cleanliness and pathogen control issues found by the FDA in April 2015, some remained. Most concerning was that the specific strain of listeria found in January 2016 was the same as the one discovered in April 2015, meaning that the company failed to address the initial infection adequately.

Finally, an inspection by the FDA pronounced Jeni's clear of all issues in June 2017. What a relief! My wife and I celebrated by going back to Jeni's and enjoying our favorites.

As a result of the three separate discoveries of the same strain of listeria and the issues with health and safety standards, the reputation of the company took a big hit. In May 2018, I presented a workshop to an executive peer advisory group in Columbus, Ohio. I asked the business leaders in the audience how they felt about Jeni's. Half said they wouldn't eat there because they associated Jeni's with listeria. That attitude is unfortunate because Jeni's has an extremely high-quality product, and the company initiated intense efforts to address the problem. Still, the stain on its reputation will take some time to fade.

So what happened? Why did Jeni's Splendid Ice Cream fail to perform splendidly on safety and sanitation? How could it open its doors in late May 2015 and shut them again in early June because of another listeria discovery? What about failing to address the same listeria contamination six months later in January 2016?

Confidence Game

The answer is both blindingly simple and stunningly complex: the **overconfidence effect,** our tendency to feel way too much confidence in our judgments.[1]

But wait, aren't leaders *supposed* to be confident? Absolutely! An attitude of confidence is critical in order to inspire followers to implement a decision made by the leader. Such motivation is a fundamental activity of leaders. Yet, wise leaders who want to protect the bottom line of their company know they need to separate exhibiting confidence during the making of decisions from implementing decisions.

During the decision-making process, it's crucial that you avoid trusting feelings of internal confidence and that you do not show confidence externally, especially if you are in a top leadership position. If you show confidence when you make decisions, it could result in your followers failing to suggest alternative options and simply following your guidance, even if they have good ideas to contribute. The result is a phenomenon known as *groupthink,* when followers simply back the leader instead of providing healthy alternative perspectives and respectful challenges.[2] According to extensive research, groupthink is one of the most important factors in major business disasters.

By contrast, once the decision is made, and mechanisms to reassess the decision at a future point are put into place, the best leaders fully commit to implementing the decision. They show confidence and inspire the troops to follow, and put their full efforts into enacting the plan. They give the decision their best shot, knowing they did a thorough job of evaluating the decision and have a process of reevaluating the decision in the future. Wise leaders, thereby, subtly balance humility during the decision-making process with confidence after the decision is made.

Here's the rub: too often, we mistakenly combine external displays of confidence when inspiring others with feeling internally confident in our own judgments. We are all human, and therefore we are fundamentally flawed in our assessments of business reality due to cognitive biases. Leaders are just as flawed as everyone else.

Unfortunately, the need to signal confidence to followers obscures the ability of leaders to see such flaws. Leaders frequently mistake the internal feeling that they experience when showing confidence outwardly—a feeling that has nothing to do with whether they assess reality accurately—with an inflated sense of their skill at parsing fact from fiction and making wise decisions. By listening to their gut, meaning the feelings they experience, rather than evaluating what's going on with their head, leaders often lose their heads —and companies suffer business disasters.

Overconfidence nearly destroyed Jeni's. Its CEO, John Lowe, said in the heat of the crisis that he thought the company wouldn't be able to survive without bankruptcy: "We threaded the needle multiple times to find financing and find backers to keep us afloat during that time."[3]

After being founded in 2002, Jeni's grew very quickly because of its truly delicious and delightful product, and a healthy company culture, which Lowe and founder Jeni Britton Bauer instituted. Sadly, its business processes of safety and sanitation did not keep up with its growth.

It's not as though Jeni's lacked warning. FDA inspections discovered serious health and safety problems in 2008. A month before the discovery of listeria in Jeni's ice cream, Blue Bell, the nation's fourth largest ice cream manufacturer, issued a major recall due to a deadly listeria outbreak.

Regrettably, Jeni's failed to do anything in response to the Blue Bell recall, which showed poor judgment and overconfidence in their own processes. That overconfidence was also evident in the health and safety issues revealed by the FDA inspections conducted after the discovery of listeria in Jeni's ice cream in late April 2015. Likewise, excessive confidence was the culprit in the premature reopening of Jeni's in late May, which resulted in another shut down in early June.

Think it's limited to Jeni's? Think again!

M&A fail to increase shareholder value—the essential measure of success for publicly traded companies—surprisingly often: between 70 to 90 percent of the time, according to different studies. Does that concern CEOs? Not much, according to a 2018 survey by Deloitte of merger and acquisition plans by CEOs.[4]

Approximately 68 percent of CEOs surveyed expected the number of deals to increase in the next year, and 63 percent expected deal size to increase compared with the previous year. More than 50 percent of CEOs at publicly traded companies claimed that the large majority of deals their company completed (more than 75 percent) have generated their expected return on investment.

A KPMG study held between 1996 and 1998 found 83 percent of mergers and acquisitions in 700 of the biggest deals failed to add to shareholder value.[5] However, 82 percent of executives in 107 companies interviewed by KPMG described their deals as successful.

There is very strong evidence, using simple before-and-after numbers, that shows returns for shareholders generally decrease after mergers and acquisitions. So why do these CEOs believe that their companies do so well? For the same reason Jeni's opened its doors way too early in May 2015: overconfidence.

Let's stop talking about CEOs and turn to another group. How about drivers?

Do you consider yourself a below-average driver, in the 1–49 percent range? What about an above-average driver, in the 50–100 percent range? Pick one.

I regularly conduct straw polls on this question in my presentations. About 80 percent of business leaders consider themselves to be above-average drivers. Interestingly, studies show that 93 percent of American college students believe they are above-average drivers as well.[6]

When rating leadership ability, 70 percent of students taking the SAT exams in 1976 rated themselves as above the median. Of the same students, 85 percent rated themselves higher than the median in regards to getting on with others, and 25 percent put themselves in the top 1 percent!

Here's another whopper: 87 percent of Stanford University MBA students rated themselves as above the median on academic performance. But it's not only students: a survey of faculty members at the University of Nebraska–Lincoln found that more than 90 percent evaluated themselves as above-average teachers.[7]

What about investors? Fun fact: Fidelity Investments reviewed the performance of its funds from 2003 through 2013, and found that the best-performing accounts belonged to investors who didn't touch their accounts during this time frame.[8]

Why? Investors have way too much confidence in their ability to predict short-term market trends, and as a result, make bad decisions that cost them money. Drivers who are overconfident make tragic decisions that put themselves and other drivers in danger. Overconfident leaders make poor decisions that often devastate the bottom lines of their organizations.

Overconfidence clearly does not serve us well in the modern world. Why did such overconfidence emerge in the ancient savanna? We're not at all confident about the evolutionary basis of the overconfidence effect, but one potential explanation has to do with reproductive success. Excessively confident people try more things and take more risks, and they both succeed and fail more often than those who take measured risks.

The successful ones might have passed on more genes in cultural contexts where the dominant male produced more children. For example, some studies suggest that perhaps 5 percent or more of the world's population is descended from the ancient conqueror Genghis Khan, due to his extraordinary ability to pass on his genes and raise his children well.

Before you consider that an argument for the benefits of overconfidence, consider what happened to all the confident rulers conquered and killed by Genghis Khan: they were the confident ones of their time who failed. By comparison, consider all the smart programmers who dropped out of college and failed to create Microsoft in the mid-1970s. How about all the entrepreneurs who started restaurants only to shut their doors and end up bankrupt a few years later? What about all the CEOs fired after failed mergers and acquisitions?

EXERCISE

Are you confident you don't need to do the exercises to get the benefits of reading this book? Then you're falling into the classic trap of overconfidence. Don't harm yourself, your career, or your business by ignoring the exercises in this chapter! Take the time to reflect on the following question for a few minutes, and write down your answer in your professional journal:

> ✐ Where have you fallen for the *overconfidence effect* in your professional activities, and how has doing so harmed you? Where have you seen other people in your organization and professional network fall for this bias in their professional activities, and how has doing so harmed them?

The Many Flavors of Overconfidence

The phrase "A little knowledge is a dangerous thing" helps explain a cognitive bias related to overconfidence called the **Dunning-Kruger effect.**[9] In this mental error, people with limited knowledge on a topic feel much more confident about their judgments compared with true experts on a topic. Experts are more likely to follow the guidance of a quote attributed to Aristotle: "The more you know, the more you know you don't know."

In the 1980s, the Dunning-Kruger effect tripped up Avon Products when the company made a number of unwise acquisitions in the health-care industry, as described in Paul Carrol and Chunka Mui's *Billion Dollar Lessons.*[10] Well known for its excellent sales in door-to-door beauty products, Avon decided to move into selling healthcare products door to door in the early 1980s. A wise decision that built on Avon's superb door-to-door sales force, the addition of health-care products resulted in strong sale growth.

It's what happened next that illustrates the Dunning-Kruger effect. After the company gained a little knowledge in the health-care field, Avon's leadership showed gross overconfidence. They acquired Foster Medical, a medical equipment-rental company, in 1984. In 1985, they bought two companies that operated nursing homes, Mediplex Group and Retirement Inns of America.

Unfortunately, Avon's leadership proved incompetent in managing these medical companies. Think "incompetence" is too strong? Think again!

In 1988, four years after the purchase, Avon took a $545 million write-off to get out of the health-care business. After they bought Mediplex for $245 million in 1985, Avon's poor management quickly turned their profitable business into one that lost money. Avon then sold Mediplex back to its previous owners for $48 million.

The owners righted the ship again and sold Mediplex in 1994 for $315 million. A pretty clear case of incompetence on the part of Avon's leadership, which should have stuck to its expertise in person-to-person selling. A little knowledge can be a dangerous thing indeed.

EXERCISE

Reflect on the following questions for a few minutes, and write down your answer in your professional journal:

📝 Where have you fallen for the ***Dunning-Kruger effect*** in your professional activities, and how has doing so harmed you? Where have you seen other people in your organization and professional network fall for this bias in their professional activities, and how has doing so harmed them?

I Knew It!

"I knew it all along." Have you heard your coworkers use that phrase when a product launch didn't succeed or a hire failed to work out? Isn't it annoying when they say that? I always want to reply, "If you knew it, why didn't you say something?"

Research finds that we vastly overestimate our prediction powers, a judgment error called ***hindsight bias***.[11] For example, scholarship finds that doctors who learned a patient's diagnosis greatly overestimated their ability to predict the diagnosis. This error leads to bad judgments—and lost lives—when doctors offer a second opinion or evaluate the difficulty of an original diagnosis.

The hindsight bias is especially harmful because doctors are less likely to admit and learn from mistakes. After all, if other doctors judge you as incompetent for delivering the wrong diagnosis (because they incorrectly think the right diagnosis was easy), you won't be very likely to admit to a mistake. Fortunately, wise hospital administrators are developing successful programs that allow doctors to acknowledge and learn from mistakes that specifically aim to counter the hindsight bias.

Companies benefit greatly from instituting similar programs. In my consulting, I've witnessed many team members blame each other for problems in projects, activities, and initiatives that didn't work out with an arrogant "I knew it all along" attitude. It didn't help them reveal and learn from mistakes.

For instance, a financial services company had their sales staff compete with each other. There's nothing wrong with some healthy competition, but the competition impeded helpful collaboration. The sales staff ripped each other for failures to make sales, saying things like, "I knew he'd never make that sale" or "Why did she waste her time on that prospect? It was obvious she was just comparison shopping."

To address this problem, we asked team members to evaluate in advance whether they think someone will make a sale or not, as well as the size of the sale. This quickly resulted in sales personnel growing less arrogant and more humble as they realized their predictions were often way off. It was one of several changes that helped encourage the sales staff to help each other, while still competing where it counted.

EXERCISE

Reflect on the following question for a few minutes, and write down your answer in your professional journal:

> ✒ Where have you fallen for **hindsight bias** in your professional activities, and how has doing so harmed you? Where have you seen other people in your organization and professional network fall for this bias in their professional activities, and how has doing so harmed them?

The Glass Is...

While I am well aware of the problems caused by the overconfidence effect and try to avoid them, I still get tripped up by a related bias to which I am particularly susceptible: *the optimism bias,* excessive confidence in a positive vision of reality.[12] Do you know people who think the glass is half full? That's me! However, in 2014, this bias ended up costing me dearly.

My wife and business partner, Agnes, and I started a nonprofit that year, Intentional Insights, dedicated to popularizing decision-making science to a broad audience. At the time, I was teaching students about these topics as a professor at Ohio State University and also consulting, coaching, and speaking for businesses. However, I wanted to reach a much broader audience in order to address the suffering caused by poor decisions for those who couldn't afford my services or didn't attend my classes. Agnes, a consultant, coach, and speaker on this topic for nonprofits, also wanted to reach a broader audience.

Prior to this, we had never collaborated professionally. Despite our love and respect for each other, it did not go smoothly. We had many fights about the future. In fact, we experienced the worst tensions in our marriage during that time.

I would suggest a promising way to reach a broad audience, and Agnes would shoot it down. I proposed people who might want to get involved, and she said they'd never do it. I offered ideas about how we could structure our business systems, and she immediately found five reasons why they wouldn't work.

I felt criticized and hurt, and she was surprised that I felt that way. It was damaging, not only for our nonprofit collaboration, but also our marriage. We felt disconnected and alienated from each other.

Finally, we confronted the issue head-on in a series of conversations, and we figured out what was going on. I tend to think the glass is half full, and she sees it half-empty. I think the grass is green on the other side, while she thinks it's yellow. I suffer from the optimism bias and she suffers from its opposite, the **pessimism bias,** excessive confidence in a negative vision of reality and strong desire to avoid risks.[13]

Finally, I understood what went on in her head and heart. As she described it, although I felt criticized and hurt when she shot down my suggestions, she thought she was protecting both of us from threats down the road. When I offered a host of suggestions, she felt anxious and threatened by each one because she saw the problems and responded defensively with her autopilot system. It didn't mean I was right or she was right; it just meant that we weren't collaborating well.

The optimism/pessimism spectrum explained the crux of the difficulties we had experienced. It was a huge breakthrough that resulted in us getting the nonprofit—and our marriage—back on track. We learned innovative ways to collaborate together for both optimists and pessimists. As a result of working those points out, we were able to join our two solo consulting, coaching, and speaking businesses into one company, Disaster Avoidance Experts, which serves businesses and nonprofits alike.

We now help clients resolve similar issues. In one instance, I was hired to help improve team collaboration in the R&D department of a midsize metal manufacturing company. One of the biggest problems stemmed from the same type of conflict that my wife and I experienced. Optimists suggested ideas and pessimists shot them down. The optimists perceived pessimists as naysayers and nitpickers; the pessimists saw optimists as always going off half-cocked and coming up with half-baked ideas.

What my wife and I did—and what worked for this company and many of my other clients—involved separating the process of creating and improving ideas. Optimists are great at generating ideas, but not good at spotting the potential flaws of each idea: they are risk blind. By contrast, pessimists don't do well at creating ideas because they see all the possible flaws of each idea. They are too risk averse, turning each molehill into a mountain.

What's the fix? Optimists create the ideas, with an understanding that they are likely too optimistic about the quality of these half-baked ideas. The optimists then hand off the ideas to the pessimists, who select the best of these ideas and finish baking them. The transformation that results is magical. The vast majority of team conflict related to idea generation disappears, and you get a united team that produces a few top-quality suggestions.

EXERCISE

Reflect on the following questions for a few minutes, and write down your answers in your professional journal:

- ✐ Where have you fallen for *optimism bias* in your professional activities, and how has doing so harmed you? Where have you seen other people in your organization and professional network fall for this bias in their professional activities, and how has doing so harmed them?

- ✐ Where have you fallen for *pessimism bias* in your professional activities, and how has doing so harmed you? Where have you seen other people in your organization and professional network fall for this bias in their professional activities, and how has doing so harmed them?

The Myth: Failing to Plan Is Planning to Fail

The phrase "Failing to plan is planning to fail" is a myth, misleading at best and actively dangerous at worst. It is important to make plans, but our gut reaction is to plan for the best outcome and ignore the high likelihood that things will go wrong. Scholars call this cognitive bias the *planning fallacy,* where we have excessive confidence that our plans will go perfectly.[14]

A more accurate phrase is, "Failing to plan *for problems* is planning to fail." To address the high likelihood that problems will crop up, you need to plan for contingencies. To do so, you have to anticipate what problems might come up and address them in advance. You also have to recognize that you can't anticipate every problem, and so you must build in a buffer of additional resources that can be deployed as unexpected problems come up.

In this example, a vice president of operations for a midsize IT firm asked me to coach a senior software engineer. Beloved by his colleagues, this engineer wanted to advance into management. However, he had difficulty completing his assigned projects on time.

After a 360-degree evaluation, it turned out that the engineer was so well loved because others came to him whenever they had challenges with their own projects. He never said no to their requests. He always thought that their requests would take just a small amount of time, yet often these "small requests" resulted in him getting deeply involved in their projects. No wonder they liked him, and no wonder he didn't get his own work done on time!

The engineer constantly fell into the planning fallacy: he thought that he would help work out a small bug, but frequently, the small bug was an indicator of a host of larger issues. We fall into the planning fallacy when we leave for a meeting that's fifteen minutes away by car exactly fifteen minutes beforehand, and forget about the possibility that we'll get stuck in traffic or forget our cell phone. As a result of such unexpected problems (which we should

learn to expect) we have unplanned costs of time, money, and reputational resources, undermining our other plans, and snowballing
into catastrophes.

It's not limited to us as individuals. Despite Germany's reputation for efficiency, the Brandenburg Willy Brandt Airport in
Berlin has cost overruns of more than three-and-half times its original budget, from the planned 2.25 billion dollars to more than 8
billion dollars and counting. Originally slated to open in 2011,
the date is now pushed back to 2021. Let's be clear: It's not simply government incompetency that's a problem. Tesla fell into the
planning fallacy with its failure to meet delivery dates for its Model
3 in 2018, hurting its reputation and profits. I remember another
example that's seared into my mind from April 1998. At a Comdex
computer industry trade show in Chicago, Microsoft's CEO Bill
Gates was demonstrating Windows 98, and the software promptly
crashed. How embarrassing!

The engineer's planning fallacy is common, and not simple
to fix. Sure, it may seem easy to say, "Well, the engineer should
have just said no," yet that approach carried its own risks, and my
awareness of my optimism made me especially sensitive to these
risks. Not only would it be very difficult for the engineer to drastically change his behavior, but it would also hurt his relationships
with other engineers. It was the quality of those relationships that
made him good managerial material. Moreover, saying no would
hurt the company's output because of the critical role the engineer
played in some high-impact projects.

Instead, I worked with the vice president of operations and
the engineer to change the engineer's job description. We agreed
that 40 percent of his activities would be directed at helping others with their projects, but no more, and that he would not get
involved in more than three such projects at a time. The revised
job description, which came with a new title and a raise, enabled
the engineer to communicate effectively to his network within the
company about his availability, and he could say no with a clear
conscience. Within nine months of the change in job description,
the engineer was promoted to management. Additionally, the company received the long-term benefit of having a new formal role for

senior engineers who spent a lot of their time informally helping others, but were not rewarded for this critical function in the past.

I coached another software engineer who successfully rose through the ranks of a software consulting company into a senior management position. He had no problem saying no, but he did not know how to engage in healthy disagreements with people who weren't computer programmers.

His intuitive approach to disagreements was to argue stridently for his own perspective, and expect others to argue for their perspectives, with the best arguments winning out. Effective among fellow software engineers, this style did was not suitable for hashing out disagreements with colleagues from the marketing, sales, and financial departments.

My client overestimated the extent to which he persuaded other people, and also the extent to which his true mental state was visible to others, an overconfidence error called the ***illusion of transparency.***[15] We worked to change his style of communication during disagreements from arguing to listening, taught him to show curiosity about the emotions and goals of others, and build up trust and mutual understanding. This approach enabled a much better resolution of disagreements, and he became increasingly acknowledged as an effective communicator and leader, eventually rising to become the company's CEO.

EXERCISE

Reflect on the following questions for a few minutes, and write down your answers in your professional journal:

- Where have you fallen for ***planning fallacy*** in your professional activities, and how has doing so harmed you? Where have you seen other people in your organization and professional network fall for this bias in their professional activities, and how has doing so harmed them?

- Where have you fallen for ***illusion of transparency*** in your professional activities, and how has doing so harmed you? Where have you seen other people in your organization and professional network fall for this bias in their professional activities, and how has doing so harmed them?

The Utility of Humility

"Humility" is a rarely heard word in business contexts. It's true that we get ahead by looking, sounding, and feeling confident—the opposite of humble.

I wouldn't dream of telling you not to look or sound confident when implementing decisions, as failing to do so would undermine your professional success. Let me remind you that what I'm asking you to do is differentiate the process of making decisions from enacting them. For you and your company to survive and thrive, it's critical for leaders—especially top leaders—to avoid feeling and showing confidence during the decision-making process. In fact, you can be much more confident in your judgments if you adopt a measure of humility about the quality of your intuitive decision-making ability, and rely instead on research-based best practices when making the decision.[16]

Once you do make the decision and put safeguards in place to reevaluate it as needed at a future point, it's full steam ahead! When you put the decision into action, that is the time to demonstrate a full-throated confidence in the decision and make sure that you and your team give the decision the best possible chance to be successful.

Probabilistic thinking offers an excellent strategy to address various aspects of overconfidence. For example, say you're in the position of Avon Products and have some limited knowledge about a new area of business you'd like to enter. Protect yourself from the Dunning-Kruger effect by using a small experiment or two to test your idea.

Avon Products charged head-first into health care, buying several companies and losing more than half a billion dollars. Wouldn't it have been much wiser to establish a couple of joint ventures, or to buy one or two nursing homes instead of a large chain? That would have provided critical information to help Avon Products learn about the low probability of success and could have saved them many hundreds of millions of dollars.

The related strategy of **making predictions about the future** easily addresses a number of dangerous judgment errors, such as hindsight bias. When I consulted with the financial services company sales team and had them evaluate the likelihood and size of sale beforehand, it greatly decreased the hindsight bias. Research shows that having doctors make a diagnosis on the available evidence before learning the actual diagnosis showed them the large extent of their overconfidence, and resulted in much more realistic evaluations

The same strategy works for calibrating optimism and pessimism. Agnes and I made a great deal of progress in our professional collaboration once we started making predictions and learning who was better calibrated. Both of us have grown much more aware of our deviations from reality (and have the satisfaction of telling the other "I told you so" when proved correct). Many of my coaching clients benefited from using this strategy to gain a more accurate perspective, as have teams with whom I worked as a consultant. For teams in particular, I find it helps to have a competitive element, with some sort of reward for the team members who make the best guess (even a small one, such as deciding on the location for the monthly office outing).

Research has shown ***considering past experiences*** is one of the best tactics to address the planning fallacy. One of the ways we addressed the problem for the software engineer involved asking him to recall how much time similar projects had taken in the past. To his credit, he recognized pretty quickly how he tended to underestimate the amount of time new projects would take. Doing so helped us come up with the new guidelines for him and other senior engineers when getting involved in other people's projects.

The Brandenburg Willy Brandt Airport delayed its opening date more than five times, and may delay it again beyond 2021. Each delay was accompanied by negative press coverage and reputational blows to its leadership, as new problems discovered shortly before each deadline forced a delay. You'd think they would learn from experience, yet unfortunately, the evidence demonstrates their continued failure to do so. Learn from their mistakes, instead of making your own, and see how you can use past experience to avoid underestimating costs of time, money, and social capital for your projects.

Jeni's also illustrates the danger of failing to consider past experiences. Let's remember that already in 2008, FDA inspections found major health and safety concerns, and just a month before the listeria discovery in Jeni's, Blue Bell issued its own listeria recall. If Jeni's applied this strategy, it could have prevented the disastrous consequences of its own listeria incident.

Yes, I'll harp again on mergers and acquisitions. If you address the dangers of overconfidence by considering the combination of past experience and probabilistic thinking about the low likelihood of success, it would make CEOs much less likely to be bullish on M&A efforts.

As for the problem of overconfidence around other people, the strategy of *considering other people's perspectives* comes in handy. To address the illusion of transparency that tripped up the software consulting company manager, I conveyed to him the value of putting himself in the shoes of those with a different mindset. I asked him to imagine what he would feel—feel, not think—if he hated arguments and shut down when facing strident disagreements.

At first, he found it difficult to develop an accurate mental model of such people. To address that, we discussed where in his life he knew people who clearly shut down in the face of disagreements. He finally recalled such situations happening frequently in his church, where he served on a committee and couldn't advance his agenda because the others failed to respond to his communication style. With that mental image, he grew more capable of modeling managers from the marketing, sales, and financial departments, and engaging with them more effectively. Moreover, he brought this experience into his church service and was able to achieve his goals in that environment as well.

The same strategy applies to addressing team conflict around optimism and pessimism bias. Showing awareness of and respect for those with opposite preferences around risk and reward helped my clients—as well as my wife and myself—make much wiser decisions to avoid threats and seize opportunities.

Getting an external perspective offers an extremely effective counterweight against overconfidence. How many times have you looked at plans drawn by your colleagues and knew immediately they'd never fit within the time and money parameters they set? Plenty of research shows that we're much more capable of seeing flaws in proposals and plans made by others than those we make. Running these plans by objective and trusted advisers, especially those who have risk and reward preferences that differ from our own, helps align our aspirations with reality. This helps if they differ from you on the optimism/pessimism spectrum, which also facilitates collaboration in team settings where optimists and pessimists tend to fight.

Last, but far from least, you can get around overconfidence by *setting policies for your future self and organization.* If you're an optimist, commit to running your plans by a pessimist, and vice versa. To address overconfidence around resources, build in more than you or your organization might need, from 20 percent for projects in areas where you're an expert to 60 percent for ones where you're not to address the Dunning–Kruger effect.

Think it's too much? Tell that to Avon Products, who wasted more than half a billion dollars. An important aspect of setting a policy for your future self and organization involves de-anchoring, going out of your comfort zone for the sake of your success. You'll be thankful when an unanticipated disaster drives your competitors into bankruptcy and you are left with more than enough to buy what remains of their resources on the auction block.

This chapter's strategies empower you to be appropriately confident, knowing when and how to have the right level of self-assurance in your abilities. In the next chapter, you will learn which issues deserve your true attention when you make important judgments.

EXERCISE

Don't be overconfident that you got what you needed from this chapter and go straight to the next one! Take a few minutes to reflect on the following questions, and write down your answers in your professional journal:

✒ How will you use *probabilistic thinking* to fight the biases described in this chapter? How will you help others in your organization and professional network use this strategy? What challenges do you anticipate in implementing this strategy and helping others do so, and what steps will you take to overcome these challenges?

☞ How will you use ***making predictions about the future*** to fight the biases described in this chapter? How will you help others in your organization and professional network use this strategy? What challenges do you anticipate in implementing this strategy and helping others do so, and what steps will you take to overcome these challenges?

☞ How will you use ***considering past experiences*** to fight the biases described in this chapter? How will you help others in your organization and professional network use this strategy? What challenges do you anticipate in implementing this strategy and helping others do so, and what steps will you take to overcome these challenges?

☞ How will you use ***considering other people's perspectives*** to fight the biases described in this chapter? How will you help others in your organization and professional network use this strategy? What challenges do you anticipate in implementing this strategy and helping others do so, and what steps will you take to overcome these challenges?

☞ How will you use ***getting an external perspective*** to fight the biases described in this chapter? How will you help others in your organization and professional network use this strategy? What challenges do you anticipate in implementing this strategy and helping others do so, and what steps will you take to overcome these challenges?

☞ How will you use ***setting a policy for your future self and organization*** to fight the biases described in this chapter? How will you help others in your organization and professional network use this strategy? What challenges do you anticipate in implementing this strategy and helping others do so, and what steps will you take to overcome these challenges?

CHAPTER SUMMARY

➦ Business leaders—and everyone else—tend to be vastly overconfident about their evaluations of reality and the quality of the decisions they make.

➦ While showing and feeling confidence is necessary when implementing decisions, we need to focus on both feeling and exhibiting humility when making decisions, especially the top leaders in an organization.

➦ Most business leaders suffer from optimism bias, the tendency to be risk blind and have excessively positive evaluations of current reality and the future. Some—especially in control functions such as finance, HR, and IT security—fall on the opposite end of the spectrum of pessimism bias, being too risk averse and down on current and future prospects.

➦ Our gut pushes us to perceive that all our business plans will go well, resulting in underestimating the amount of time and money required and budgeted, so that a myriad of predictable problems results in an avoidable crises.

➦ Our instinct is to overestimate the extent to which other people understand what we feel and think, as well as the meaning we intend to convey with our words.

➦ Addressing overconfidence-related judgment errors requires deploying the following techniques:
  » probabilistic thinking
  » making predictions about the future
  » considering past experiences
  » considering other people's perspectives
  » getting an external perspective
  » setting a policy for your future self and organization

Chapter 6

Are You Paying Attention?

Chapter Key Benefits

✿ Develop an appreciation of the problems that
stem from allowing our gut reaction to determine
the object of our attention.

✿ Learn the dangerous judgment errors that result
from paying attention to the wrong thing at the
wrong time or in the wrong way.

✿ Place into our arsenal needed techniques to
manage the cognitive biases that result from
attention-related judgment errors.

One of our most valuable resources is our attention. Yet, if we don't apply this resource effectively, we can lose many other resources: time, money, social capital, and so on. Research shows that when we are intentional in how we deploy our attention we can avoid disasters of all sorts.

While I learned the theory behind the dangerous judgment errors associated with attention in graduate school many years ago, I felt it on my own skin more recently. My own judgment error occurred when I hired a graphic designer to create the layout and graphics for a booklet that included an assessment called "Dangerous Judgment Errors in the Workplace" (you'll see the assessment in the next chapter).

My preference is to hire vendors through recommendations from my professional contact network. Unfortunately, no one knew a designer with experience in booklet layouts. So I went on *Upwork. com,* a website I use to hire virtual contractors for various virtual tasks when I can't find one through personal references.

In my request for proposals, I said I'd provide the text and some samples of booklet layouts and graphics I liked, and then have the contractor come up with the final design that matched some of the other booklets they designed in the past. I asked the graphic designers to provide links to booklet layouts and graphics in their portfolios, so I could be sure I liked their design styles.

My proposal received dozens of bids. I communicated with a number of potential vendors and evaluated the quality and thoroughness of their communication. Finally, I selected one: not the cheapest bid, but the one with a highly impressive portfolio and great communication. I believed this contractor would do a quality job to match the high standards we have at Disaster Avoidance Experts, while also being easy to work with, saving me time and energy.

As you might have guessed by now, my expectations weren't matched by what happened in reality. The problem? Designing the layout and graphics for a booklet is a task that involves a great deal of detailed work. The graphic designer, whose portfolio featured great work, repeatedly made small mistakes and failed to follow directions.

For example, the assessment has thirty questions, and I asked him to standardize the graphic style of the questions. When he sent me the rough draft, I found that about one-third had some sort of issue with the layout. I felt frustrated. Why didn't he *see* the obvious graphic design problems? I asked him to fix the mistakes, but he only fixed about half of them, with five questions still screwed up. I went through all the questions, and specifically pointed out all the problems, numbering them one through five. He fixed three of the five. I asked him to fix the remaining two, and then he did so.

The same song and dance went on for the rest of the sections of the assessment. If I hadn't prepaid for the project (per the terms of Upwork), I would have found someone else. Yet it was too late at that point, as incompetence doesn't violate the terms of the contract. Heck, I would have left the money as sunken costs, yet I knew the time and effort it would take to get another graphic designer was not worth it.

I'll be honest: I'm not a detail-oriented person. I'm best at the 30,000-feet-in-the-air level. Moreover, I get frustrated quickly when I see incompetence and stupidity (which makes it difficult for me to deal with government bureaucracy).

Fortunately, my wife and business partner, Agnes, is better at those things, so I got her involved. She's more detail oriented and patient when dealing with people, which is why she makes the vast majority of customer service calls for our business. She was also pretty frustrated with the innumerable small mistakes made by the vendor, but dealt with it better than I did.

Eventually, we got the assessment booklet done to the high-quality standards that we have at Disaster Avoidance Experts. Yet getting the graphic designer to do little things and address the problems was like squeezing blood from a stone. It sucked up a surprising amount of time from Agnes and I, and caused us both a lot of stress, frustration, and anxiety.

Later, when I evaluated the problems that occurred to learn from the situation, as I do after every failure on my part, I realized I paid attention to the wrong things when I looked for a graphic designer. Specifically, I focused on the information I had available and considered important and impressive: the emotionally appealing graphic designs in the contractor's portfolio, and the speed and thoroughness of his communication.

Indeed, the vendor had technical competence in execution, but terrible detail orientation and ability to follow instructions. Those two soft-skill failures don't come through in his initial communication or portfolio, which had plenty of quality work. In fact, he eventually added the booklet he designed for me to his portfolio. It made me wonder if all those other clients whose work he added to his portfolio had to struggle to get him to do a good job.

As a result of that situation, I learned to pay attention to important elements of a situation, project, or person that aren't immediately obvious. From now on, when I hire someone who shows me examples of their previous work, I look for the best samples in that person's portfolio and request to speak to those references. I ask those people what they liked about working with this person and what could have been improved. If I had done that in the first place, I would have saved a lot of time, energy, stress, and negative emotions.

Attention Retention

What I fell for with the graphic designer is a cognitive bias called **attentional bias,** a dangerous judgment error in which we tend to pay attention to the most emotionally salient factors in our immediate environment—the ones that feel like they are the most critical—whether or not they're actually the most important ones.1 Attentional bias causes us to forget that other factors beyond what we're seeing are important too, as I did with the vendor. It can also cause us to overemphasize the importance of emotionally arousing elements in our surroundings.

When I was hired to improve the internal and external risk management processes for a biotech start-up, I noticed a problem in the boardroom. The two cofounders failed to get along with each other on a regular basis. They engaged in destructive conflict over frequently minor issues. Now, constructive conflict—during which you debate anything from the strategic questions of the company's future to tactical issues about how to get there—can be very healthy, as long as it doesn't bleed over into destructive conflict, with the focus turning to personalities and cliques.

I learned from other employees that the cofounders came from an entrepreneurial culture, so they didn't have the experience to work out problems diplomatically in a healthy conflict, which is necessary for business leaders in most Fortune 1000 companies. Technical geniuses, the cofounders lacked important soft leadership skills including social intelligence, which is the ability to evaluate and influence other people's emotions and relationships. As the start-up grew bigger, they had to address more and more significant issues. They didn't have a healthy approach to hashing out divergent visions.

Senior employees that were hired from bigger companies lacked the political power to address the issue head-on, and the cofounders didn't read their indirect hints well. One of these employees, the chief risk officer who hired me as a consultant, suggested to the two cofounders that their conflictual relations represented a risk. So, he proposed that we meet to see if the situation could be improved. As an external consultant, if I pissed off one or both of the cofounders, it was only a four-month consulting contract that was on the line, not my job in the company.

When I got the two of them together, I asked why they originally wanted to start the company. They both passionately described the problem their company was trying to fix and how none of the existing biotech companies had the unique solution they offered. Next, I asked what brought the two of them together to found the company. With some initial reluctance, they described the value that the other person brought to their partnership. I then asked them to outline what they agreed on regarding the strategy and the tactics of the company. After that, I asked them to outline areas of disagreement, both strategic and tactical. Both expressed some surprise that their strategic vision overlapped almost completely, and that they differed in only two out of twenty-seven tactical areas.

Following that, we talked about how with their extensive history, their monumental accomplishments in building the start-up to many millions in revenue and several dozen employees, and overwhelming agreement on strategy and tactics, it was a shame that their conflicts in the boardroom were so divisive. Both of them acknowledged being headstrong personalities who sometimes let their passion in the heat of the moment overcome their common sense and diplomacy.

After that, I brought up the problem of attentional bias in conflicts, where we often tend to focus on the 1 percent on which we disagree and disregard the 99 percent on which we agree. We talked about how the area of disagreement feels more important and authentic to our gut, even though objectively it's not. They both agreed that they made this dangerous judgment error many times during disagreements with each other.

They committed to focus and remember the areas of agreement during disagreements. We came up with a nonverbal signal that they could use to remind them: raising nine fingers on their hands, as a reminder of "99 percent agreement." When I checked in a year later, the two cofounders were still doing well together, and the start-up's revenue had grown by more than 80 percent.

It's easy to understand the attentional bias from an evolutionary perspective. In the ancient savanna, paying excessive attention to emotionally salient features of our environment proved crucial for survival. Emotions that caused us to jump when we saw a sudden movement on the ground saved our ancestors from snakes and other dangerous creatures. It was better for our survival to jump at a thousand shadows than be bitten by one snake. Similarly, perceiving conflict as a huge threat was critical for people living in tribes because being thrown out of a tribe usually meant certain death. We are no longer in that environment. Still, our emotions act like we are. When you follow your gut it will result in losing money, time, social capital, and other resources because you pay attention to the wrong things in the wrong manner at the wrong time.

EXERCISE

Pay attention to where you might make attention mistakes by doing this and all the other exercises in this chapter. Reflect on the following questions for a few minutes, and write down your answers in your professional journal:

- ✐ Where have you fallen for *attentional bias* in your professional activities, and how has doing so harmed you? Where have you seen other people in your organization and professional network fall for this bias in their professional activities, and how has doing so harmed them?

What Gets Measured Gets Managed?

The well-known business saying "What gets measured gets managed" contains a lot of wisdom. However, like many wise sayings, it can be taken too far and make us excessively complacent. The problem is an attention-related cognitive bias called **surrogation,** our tendency to equate the measure that we're using with the outcome that we want to measure.[2]

Surrogation can get us into a lot of trouble. Say you're going to host an important prospect who is coming to town to evaluate whether you'd be a good vendor for his needs. You ask your executive assistant to find a good restaurant. The assistant checks out the *Yelp.com* reviews and reserves a restaurant with great reviews. When you get there, you find the food overdone and overpriced, and the service to be just a bit faster than a snail's pace. Later, you read an article about how that restaurant was caught paying a shady marketing company to improve its Yelp and other online reviews. A classic case of surrogation: you thought that reviews measured quality of food and customer service, but the restaurant fudged the numbers.

Perhaps you're too smart for that. Well, here's a situation that happened to a coaching client of mine, a regional manager of a large retail chain. In one of our coaching conversations a couple of years ago, she brought up something that was bugging her. The retail chain conducted monthly employee satisfaction surveys. Stores that had higher employee satisfaction almost invariably had higher employee retention. Store managers were rewarded with bonuses for improving and maintaining high employee satisfaction.

However, a few months ago, she noticed a weird dynamic in a store in her region. Employee satisfaction increased in those stores, but employee retention decreased. She didn't pay too much attention at first, thinking it an outlier situation, but the trend persisted.

I advised her to investigate the details of how employee satisfaction was measured. She pushed back and said the survey was anonymous and conducted by email, so there would be no way to mess with it. Still, I persisted, and pointed out surrogation as a cognitive bias that makes us too confident in our measurement systems.

It turned out that one store manager created an effective strategy to mess with the employee satisfaction survey process. He tied the bonuses that employees in his store received (which he controlled) to the ratings on the employee satisfaction survey. Doing so didn't go against the letter of company policy, but of course went against the spirit of the survey. His actions resulted in store staff pressuring each other to give unrealistically high employee satisfaction ratings. The store manager got a higher bonus for his employees reporting higher satisfaction and also put less effort into ensuring that employees actually felt satisfied. As a result, the store's employee retention naturally decreased, both because of his lesser efforts to improve employee satisfaction and because of the discomfort of the more ethical employees.

The regional manager, upon finding this out, disciplined the store manager. Yet, as I gently pointed out to her, part of this was her fault. She focused her messaging to her store managers on customer service. A very important message, no doubt, and a bit too much of a good thing at the same time. She did not provide adequate leadership to convey the importance of long-term employee satisfaction to store success. She resolved to do better in the future, and also reported the employee satisfaction incident so the company policy could be adjusted to prevent future problematic out-of-the-box thinking by store managers.

EXERCISE

Reflect on the following questions for a few minutes, and write down your answers in your professional journal:

✐ Where have you fallen for *surrogation* in your professional activities, and how has doing so harmed you? Where have you seen other people in your organization and professional network fall for this bias in their professional activities, and how has doing so harmed them?

It's No Hyperbole

Like the store manager who undermined the employee satisfaction survey, we too often exchange higher long-term gains for smaller short-term ones. Scholars use the term *hyperbolic discounting* for this dangerous judgment error, highlighting that we excessively discount value in the future for the pressing urge of what we want right now.[3]

This tendency happens at all levels within organizations, including the highest ones. Think back to the creative accounting that brought down Enron. Under pressure from quarterly earnings reports to Wall Street, and worried about losing high status from Enron's previous success, its leadership pushed the accounting department to falsify Enron's books. The game couldn't continue for too long, and those leaders knew it, but they still pursued a course that eventually landed them in the headlines for all the wrong reasons, and then in jail.

More broadly, quarterly earnings are a frequent complaint for prominent business leaders and investors who are concerned with the short-term focus showed by most CEOs. People like Jamie Damon, the CEO of JPMorgan Chase; Bob Lutz, a former executive at Ford, General Motors, and Chrysler; and Warren Buffet, CEO of Berkshire Hathaway, have all called for the abolition of the quarterly guidance by companies. A focus on quarterly earnings inhibits long-term planning and causes CEOs to focus on maximizing immediate profit goals, which drives up stock price in the short term while harming a company's bottom line down the road.

What kind of critical issues get left behind with excessive focus on the short term? At the most fundamental level, emphasizing the immediate level makes it hard for organizations to invest into organizational change. Any organizational change will involve short-term resource investments for the sake of long-term gains. In the large majority of cases, such future benefits will not show up in the next quarter's earnings. Thus, resources that could have been invested into boosting earnings instead go into changing the organization. It takes strong and intelligent leadership both to recognize and push through initiatives that delay short-term profits for long-term positive change.

As a rule of thumb, an organization should spend at least 10 percent and generally no more than 20 percent of its resources working on the business, rather than in the business. "Working *in* the business" refers to anything related directly to external output, such as creating your product or service, marketing and selling it to clients, and post-sale customer service. "Working *on* the business" means improving the way your organization conducts its business, such as professional development for leaders and employees, developing and improving internal processes and measurements, and conducting strategic and tactical planning. The latter usually don't show up in quarterly earnings reports, but show up a year down the road in improved earnings and result higher stock prices.

Why the large range, from 10 to 20 percent? The key is to time your work on the business wisely and match the current situation in your company as well as broader market conditions.

The most strategic and experienced business leaders know that they need to put the most effort into working on the business during good and quiet times for the company. It may sound counterintuitive to do so, but then this whole book is counterintuitive, right?

Consider why periods of healthy company growth and calm external environment represent the best times to work on the business. It's easiest to find resources for improving your company when you're not in the midst of a crisis situation and your balance sheet looks healthy.

You can also plan ahead effectively for working on the business. If you're a publicly traded company, you can give slightly lower earnings guidance to account for additional investment into working on the business; privately held companies and nonprofits can include such work in their annual budgets. By doing this work, an organization will minimize potential threats and be most prepared to seize unexpected opportunities, as well as figure out the best places to decrease costs and increase revenue.

Yet even in the midst of harsh market conditions or a crunch time for your company, you don't want to stop process and people improvements completely, although you might want to decrease such work. Otherwise, you'll have a heck of a time restarting the process later. Working on the business has a great deal of momentum involved, and you'll lose a lot of gains by stopping the process.

The best strategy to work on your business involves an explicit ability to ramp up and scale down depending on market conditions and your company's current situation. For instance, I consulted for a manufacturing company with about 1,400 employees on setting up a leadership development system. Previously, it had an ad-hoc leadership development process, dependent on when the C-suite decided to do a retreat or when local leaders sought out their own professional development for themselves and their employees.

With the new system, its ninety or so frontline leaders get together for a mutual learning retreat one day a month on average. Each learning retreat day involves several elements. The company's executives present a brief report on the health of the company and progress against goals from the strategic plan. Next, in small groups, the frontline leaders discuss ideas for strategy and innovation, and present the most worthwhile ideas as selected by the group. After that, they get back into small groups to learn best practices from each other and problem-solve issues each one experienced, with another presentation about what each small group judged most important. Next, an outside speaker presents to help the frontline leaders learn new ideas from external best practices. Afterward, small groups discuss how the speaker's content might benefit their everyday activities, with reporting out of the best ideas. The day concludes with a social event to build community and mutual trust among the leadership. In addition, each frontline leader takes an average of half a day a month for professional development on their own, whether that involves going to relevant conferences, meeting with a coach, taking online courses, and so on. (They receive funds to do so.)

Then, the frontline leaders invest two days per month into using this information to improve processes and professional development for their teams. They take half a day per month to gather their team for a mini-retreat. There, the frontline leader reports on the team's progress against strategic goals and also on what they thought most useful to the team from the leadership retreat day. Next, they have team members discuss how to integrate the best ideas from the leadership retreat into their activities and improve processes. They also have their team generate ideas for innovations and best practices, and conclude with a social event. Sometimes, they have an outside speaker. For the weeks without a mini-retreat, the team conducts an hour-long meeting during which they problem-solve various issues that come up. The frontline leaders then bring what they see as the most helpful ideas and problems they couldn't easily solve themselves, or think might benefit from broader discussion, to the monthly leadership retreat.

The rest of the team's professional development and process improvement time of a day and a half per month is up to each individual manager. It depends on their team's needs and goals, with some funding dedicated for group training activities. Furthermore, the company gives each employee half a day per month and some money for individual professional development based on the employee's personal priorities.

With this system, each frontline leader spends on average three and a half days per month on professional development and process improvement, which represents just over 15 percent of the average of twenty-two working days per month; each employee spends about two-and-a-half days a month on these activities, so just over 10 percent. The beauty of this system involves a combination of some standardized professional development and process improvement practices across the organization with flexibility for each team, leader, and employee to pursue additional learning and improvement based on local and personal needs and goals.

Moreover, the system provides the ability to scale up and down depending on the economic situation of the company and broader market conditions. When things are going well and the company is not busy, the leadership schedules additional time for learning retreats, making them two days instead of one, and devoting the whole second day for an external speaker to conduct a day-long seminar. When things aren't going as well, whether that means a decrease in available resources or during a busy season for the company, the company reduces the learning retreats to half a day instead of a whole day. The same kind of dynamic occurs at the frontline level in the teams themselves.

Additionally, the learning system offers flexibility in scheduling for different kinds of teams. A case in point, if the company's production facilities weren't operating at desired capacity due to insufficient orders from customers, the manufacturing frontline leaders and employees spend more time doing professional development and process improvement, while the marketing and sales team focuses more on promoting the company's products and making sales.

To ensure effective management of this learning system, the company's chief learning officer implemented and adjusted the system as needed. I later learned she added semiannual executive retreats for the C-suite as a part of this system. With this combination of flexibility and standardization, the company's top leaders succeeded in overcoming the hyperbolic discounting that undercuts the long-term success of many organizations in working on the business.

EXERCISE

Reflect on the following question for a few minutes, and write down your answers in your professional journal:

> ✏️ Where have you fallen for *hyperbolic discounting* in your professional activities, and how has doing so harmed you? Where have you seen other people in your organization and professional network fall for this bias in their professional activities, and how has doing so harmed them?

Ignorance Is No Excuse!

A dangerous judgment error called *omission bias* refers to when you evaluate the negative consequences of not taking an action as less bad than the negative consequences of taking an action.[4] If you're a philosophy fan, you might be familiar with the quote from philosopher William James: "When you have to make a choice and don't make it, that is in itself a choice." This refers to the omission bias.

I fondly remember shopping at Circuit City for my computer needs at the start of the millennium, as I was completing graduate school at the University of North Carolina at Chapel Hill while moonlighting as a consultant and coach. It was distressing to see the headlines in November 2008 that Circuit City declared bankruptcy, although I got a few good deals at the going-out-of-business sale at my local store. I decided to investigate further and found that the most crucial reason for Circuit City's bankruptcy stemmed from its leadership, especially CEO Phillip Schoonover. The leadership failed to act in a timely manner to address the crisis in flat-panel TV sales throughout the last several years. Its executive team focused a critical part of the Circuit City revenue model around selling flat-panel televisions and accessories such as speakers, cables, and brackets, as well as extended warranties. (As I mentioned earlier in the book, extended warranties are not worth the investment.) While flat-panel TVs sold at Circuit City for $2,400 in the fall of 2005, only a year later, Walmart and Costco offered them for $995, severely undercutting Circuit City's business model, both in the margins for flat-panel TVs and accessories.

Schoonover acknowledged his failure to heed clear warning signs that the bottom would drop out of flat-panel TV sales, and tried to deal with the drastic revenue drop through a wide variety of measures.[5] Unfortunately, one of his decisions involved cutting wages and laying off experienced (and better-paid) staff, which resulted in a drastic drop in morale, bad PR, and slower sales. Schoonover resigned in September 2008, two months before Circuit City entered bankruptcy proceedings. Failing to heed warning signs and make wise choices while Circuit City still had time—and cash—resulted in bad crisis judgment under pressure, and the eventual bankruptcy of the number two appliance retailer in the United States.

Have you ever heard the phrase "Fiddling while Rome burns"? The phrase refers to the supposed story that Roman emperor Nero played the fiddle while Rome burned during the great fire of CE 64. The story is false—what we call fake news nowadays—but nevertheless the phrase refers to occupying yourself with unimportant but simple matters while you neglect more important but complex priorities. This too-common judgment error bears the name *bikeshedding,* also known as *Parkinson's law of triviality.*[6]

Perhaps you've sat through a boring meeting during which a long-winded colleague focused the group's attention on some unimportant matter while critical issues got ignored. Or perhaps those in the meeting drilled down deep into a trivial matter while they let key but complex topics go by. As an example, I sat in on a client's C-suite meeting during which leadership discussed the online marketing strategy proposed by the marketing team. The top leaders got into the minute details of messing around with the design of the website home page and spent about an hour on that topic.

Unfortunately, they only gave a few minutes to the much more important but complex matter of the variety of strategies to get clients to visit the website. It's much easier to pass judgment on the location and content of tabs on the top row of the website than inbound marketing, yet building a nice website won't matter if it doesn't get visitors. I was hired to address a different matter and chose not to bring up this issue, even though I thought the marketing department's strategy for bringing clients to the website was wrong. Indeed, my client ended up revising the marketing strategy after six months, when their website visitors were 60 percent below projections.

EXERCISE

Reflect on the following questions for a few minutes, and write down your answers in your professional journal:

- ☞ Where have you fallen for *omission bias* in your professional activities, and how has doing so harmed you? Where have you seen other people in your organization and professional network fall for this bias in their professional activities, and how has doing so harmed them?

- ☞ Where have you fallen for *bikeshedding* in your professional activities, and how has doing so harmed you? Where have you seen other people in your organization and professional network fall for this bias in their professional activities, and how has doing so harmed them?

Don't Argue With Success?

One of the most challenging and counterintuitive cognitive biases, *outcome bias* refers to the dangerous judgment error of judging decisions by paying attention to their outcomes rather than focusing on the process of making the decision.[7] In my consulting, coaching, and speaking experience, business leaders struggle with the concept that they should occasionally argue with success and sometimes reward failure. After all, companies almost always reward decision-makers by the outcome of their decisions, such as a CEO for her investment into a profitable new product category or an investment portfolio manager for the growth of his portfolio.

Successful people are uncomfortable with the realization that luck sometimes plays a much larger role in the success of decision-makers than skill. The best that decision-makers can do is maximize the possibility of success, and then roll the dice. The wisest course of action—the one most likely to produce the best incentives for future success—is to reward decision-makers for how well they maximized the possibility of success, regardless of the outcome of their decision.

To demonstrate the danger of rewarding outcomes over process, let's use portfolio managers as an example. Imagine you know someone who has outperformed the stock market for more than a decade, and he offers you a chance to invest into his private, exclusive mutual fund. Would you do it? Most people would say yes, and gladly make the investment of their hard-earned cash.

Let's dig deeper. Say there are 100,000 portfolio managers who operate simply based on random blind luck. Throughout the course of a year, 50,000 would underperform the broad stock market and 50,000 would outperform the market. The next year, out of the 50,000 who outperformed the market, 25,000 would underperform the market, and 25,000 would outperform the market. If this trend continued for ten years, you'd find that by the end of a decade, fifty portfolio managers would outperform the market by blind luck alone.

What would happen then? They'd make the headlines in *Forbes, Fortune,* CNBC, and elsewhere as the stock gurus of the decade. They'd write bestselling books about their stock-picking strategies: *How I Went with My Gut and Beat the Odds.* Money would flow into the mutual funds they manage.

Yet next year, twenty-five of them would underperform the market, and twenty-five would outperform it. The situation is similar to having 100,000 people toss a coin ten times each. Fifty of them on average will get all heads, like the portfolio managers who have ten good years in a row; there's no guarantee that they will be lucky next year. Indeed, research strongly suggests that the vast majority of mutual funds are not worthwhile investments, and seeming success results simply from random statistical fluctuations, meaning luck.[8] Yet outcome bias results in all sorts of made-up stories about portfolio managers who are geniuses at picking stocks.

Luck also plays a role, although a smaller one, in business decision-making. You know this. You've certainly worked on projects where you did everything right, made the best choices possible and implemented them as well as you could, only to have circumstances outside your control wipe out all your hard work. By contrast, how often did you make choices that, looking back, you'd consider subpar? Or perhaps you made some implementation mistakes, only to have some good luck come along to help you out and save the day?

Happens to all of us, right? We're not perfect; we're human.

Luck plays the smallest role in organizational settings on the lower levels. On the front lines, where the rubber meets the road, the consequences of decisions usually reveal themselves very quickly. Is your client satisfied with the customer service you provided or not? Did you make the sale or not? Has the online advertisement driven sufficient traffic to the website or not? Does the website convert prospects into joining the email list or not? It's easy to repeat the steps or tweak the process on the front lines, and learn to do better going forward. As a result, frontline employees and their immediate supervisors get valuable experience that improves their future decision-making.

The higher up the food chain you go, the longer it takes for strategic decision-making to play out. What's going to be the consequence of a strategic partnership? Will the newly hired CEO take the company in the right direction? Is outsourcing to China or the Philippines the best option? Only time will tell, and it often takes years rather than months for the outcomes of decisions to be revealed. Moreover, strategic decision-making is more vulnerable to luck than frontline work because many more factors impact strategic decisions. Finally, due to these long-term cycles, the decision-maker might have moved on to another role before the consequences of their decision fully impacts the company.

As a result, it's critical to evaluate decision-making at the managerial and especially executive level by the process used to reach a decision. Did the decision-maker(s) take the steps needed to avoid dangerous judgment errors and maximize the decision's likelihood of success? If so, their performance deserves to be rewarded and incentivized, regardless of the outcome. The outcome should not be ignored, of course, because it provides valuable evidence about the quality of the process. Still, the role of luck in the outcome needs to be considered as a critical factor in the incentive structure if we want to create truly successful organizations.

I present this point toward the end of my half-day or full-day workshops, after laying the groundwork with less controversial and more easily graspable concepts. It's often at this point in my talks that the senior business leaders in the audience cross their arms and adopt a defensive posture.

I understand their feelings, as I felt the same way when I learned about the outcome bias. I think of myself as highly successful, so it was rough to realize that luck had a significant role in my success.

What helped these business leaders lower their defenses and accept the concept was reminding them of the many failures of highly competent, smart executives. Pretty much every CEO and their C-suite team consists of people who worked for many years to make their way to the top, on the basis of top-notch performance when they were climbing the corporate ladder. Unfortunately, a number of CEOs who were celebrated at one time ended up castigated later for a series of mistakes that either undermined or destroyed their companies, such as Bernard Ebbers at WorldCom, Chuck Conway at Kmart, John Rigas at Adelphia Communications, Juergen Schrempp at DaimlerChrysler, Kay Whitmore at Eastman Kodak, and many others.

At the height of their careers, these business giants stood at the forefront of their industries; yet how the might have fallen. Their examples provide an invaluable lesson in humility and disaster avoidance for the rest of us. We can't rest on our laurels. We need to do everything possible to improve the quality of our decisions, rather than believing that our past success will guarantee our future success.

A related cognitive bias that confounds our intuitions when we evaluate success and failure is known as ***survivorship bias.*** This happens when we pay attention only to the information that survived to reach us and fail to consider the information that did not.[9] You know all those books written by or about successful business leaders and companies? The message they convey: follow the steps of these ultra-successful folks and companies, and you're golden!

Unfortunately, there are hidden dangers in doing so. First, you don't know which of these leaders and companies are truly successful. The CEOs and companies I listed as dismal failures were once celebrated as business geniuses. Even ones who succeeded during their business careers might have made choices that doomed the future of their companies. For instance, former CEO of GE Jack Welch, who headed the company from 1981 to 2001, saw its share price grow 4,000 percent under his leadership.[10] Yet, his handpicked successor, Jeffrey Immelt, made a series of problematic decisions that resulted in a stock price drop of more than 30 percent and was pushed to retire in the summer of 2018. Welch placed most of the blame for the company's poor performance on Immelt. Given that Welch personally chose Immelt, some of the blame for these failures resides with Welch, which negatively colors his reign as a CEO.

Second, you don't know which of the decisions by these leaders and companies actually led to their success. After all, both luck and context—being at the right place at the right time with the right people—plays a large role in success. To know which decisions led to success with confidence, you need to have information about what would have happened if they made different decisions.

While that's impossible, we can look at other unsuccessful companies and leaders in a relatively similar position and compare their decisions to those who succeeded. For example, I'd love to see a book that compares the success of Best Buy to the failure of Circuit City, or the success of Facebook to the failure of MySpace.

However, it's very rare to see a book written about failures, because readers aren't interested in knowing about them. A typical case of survivorship bias; most readers don't recognize the value of understanding why something failed, as they focus only on emulating success. By contrast, the wisest business leaders know that they and their companies will fail, and their most important job is to avoid failure. For example, in a November 2018 meeting with employees,

Amazon CEO Jeff Bezos stated, "Amazon is not too big to fail. In fact, I predict one day Amazon will fail. Amazon will go bankrupt. If you look at large companies, their lifespans tend to be thirty-plus years, not a hundred-plus years. . . . We have to try and delay that day for as long as possible."[11] There's a leader who knows the importance of studying failure, and in turn tries to prevent it (or at least delay it).

Although one-to-one comparisons of failure and success are valuable, there's a better way to obtain the critically important information about what brings true success: assessing a number of companies and leaders in the same industry and/or with similar characteristics to figure out best and worst practices. That's what behavioral economists do when they use large data sets to evaluate wise and poor decision-making strategies by individuals and companies. This research forms both the basis for this book and all of our consulting, coaching, speaking, and other services and products at Disaster Avoidance Experts

An example involves circumventing the problem of survivorship bias by helping a consulting client figure out important information that doesn't survive unless you deliberately look for the information. A direct-to-consumer retailer wanted to learn more about customers who stopped purchasing its products, but its customer satisfaction surveys didn't provide useful information. After all, the customer satisfaction survey only conveyed information about existing (surviving) customers, not those who did not survive. To address this issue, we created a "Customer Dissatisfaction Survey" and sent it to former customers. We also included an incentive of a chance to win a new laptop as well as a coupon from the company if the customer completed the survey. The retailer received very valuable information about why customers left. There were reasons under the company's control, such as website usability issues and problematic customer service experiences, in addition to factors not under my client's control, such as customers whose economic situation changed. Such information would not have survived to reach the company through typical channels. As a bonus, the coupon encouraged a fraction of those who filled out the survey to re-engage with the company.

EXERCISE

Reflect on the following questions for a few minutes, and write down your answers in your professional journal:

☞ Where have you fallen for *outcome bias* in your professional activities, and how has doing so harmed you? Where have you seen other people in your organization and professional network fall for this bias in their professional activities, and how has doing so harmed them?

☞ Where have you fallen for *survivorship bias* in your professional activities, and how has doing so harmed you? Where have you seen other people in your organization and professional network fall for this bias in their professional activities, and how has doing so harmed them?

Solving Attention Judgment Errors

One of the most effective techniques to solve attention-related cognitive biases involves *considering alternative explanations and options.* When you focus on this, you can immediately turn your attention to aspects of the issue at hand that are not immediately visible or don't have the gut feeling of importance.

The Customer Dissatisfaction Survey represents one clear way to consider such alternative, not immediately visible information. By implementing that survey, my client received insights regarding the concerns of former customers that caused them to stop purchasing the company's products. Without such knowledge, the client would have not been able to learn about and address the factors under its control. However, after my client gained this knowledge, they worked to develop customer service by improving both wages and quality controls among its call center staff, as well as improving website design.

On an individual level, review your major decisions during the last few years and consider the alternative by evaluating what would have happened if luck didn't go your way or vice versa. How would your business and career be different? Then, reflect on what you can do to luck-proof your decisions in the future, by minimizing downsides if luck doesn't go your way and maximizing upside if it does. If you are in a leadership role in an organization, what systems can you create that luck-proof decisions?

Probabilistic thinking offers another excellent way to address attention judgment errors and reward wise decision-making. For instance, after I gave a speech at a technology conference, the chief operations officer of a database company recognized that her firm's sales incentive system relied too much on luck because it rewarded those who exceed monthly quotas. In their existing system, a salesperson could hit a monthly quota by catching a break with one big sale to a large client and take it easy the rest of the month when all the quotas zeroed out.

Moreover, sales staff did not have accountability for post-sale customer experience, which created incentives to make sales of expensive database products that might not be the best fit for the customer's needs. The customer often figured out that the database, while performing to specifications, failed to match the purpose for which they purchased it. Yet the customer's dissatisfaction was not reflected in the sales staff compensation plan, despite the harm to the company's reputation and bottom line of such outcomes.

The system exemplified the faults of outcome bias by rewarding luck over wise decision-making, and making the big sale over making the right sale. Disaster Avoidance Experts worked with the company to luck-proof the sales compensation plan and make it probable that the sales staff would sell customers what they truly needed. We changed the compensation structure from simply rewarding outcomes to rewarding staff who took the appropriate steps needed to maximize the probability of making the right sale to the right client. To do so, we looked at the typical behaviors of sales staff who outperformed others consistently both in exceeding their sales quote and in the lowest number of complaints post-sale. Then, we crystallized these behaviors into a model for the rest to follow.

The model had a series of steps that ranged from building a relationship and figuring out true customer needs to checking in three and six months after the sale to see how the database addressed customers' needs. The plan included sales staff documenting the steps. Performance evaluations and bonuses depended on three factors: 1) following the sales model; 2) making the sale; and 3) high customer satisfaction six months after the sale. That way, good salespeople who got into unlucky streaks could still be rewarded for following desired behaviors. In turn, failures in making sales or high customer complaints could be addressed by sales managers who checked whether the salesperson actually followed the model. Often, it turned out that crucial steps were skipped, and the sales manager then coached the salesperson on following the model. Throughout the next twelve months, both sales and customer satisfaction increased by more than 15 percent.

The related strategy of **making predictions about the future** helps address judgment errors such as bikeshedding. Before going into the weeds of making a decision or evaluation a proposal, it's useful to discuss what you perceive as the more and less important aspects of the issue at hand. Then, you can choose to invest your time and energy on the most important ones, even if you are tempted to argue about website home page tabs rather than discuss the complexities of inbound marketing strategy.

Likewise, it's important to place red flags on your predictions of future market conditions, especially ones most important for your business model. Circuit City's leadership failed to do so in its flat-panel TV pricing predictions. As a result, the shareholders and employees paid the price for the leadership's failure when Circuit City went bankrupt because of unwise crisis decision-making.

By **considering past experiences** with similar activities, you can address various attention judgment errors. For instance, when I reflect on my experience with the graphic designer it motivates me to ask for references and focus my attention on soft skills necessary for good collaboration with a vendor, regardless of technical competence. The store manager finessing the employee satisfaction survey made the district manager much more aware of how the retail chain's business systems might be undercut by employees for their own benefit.

The temptation to take shortcuts for immediate profit over much larger long-term gains can be addressed by the technique of **considering the long-term future and repeating scenarios.** The creative accounting that brought down leading business figures—often under pressure from quarterly reports—could have been addressed through this strategy because it would have inevitably been discovered. On a broader societal level, the subprime mortgage crisis of 2008 resulted from chasing short-term gains that would inevitably be undone when house prices collapsed.

Within an individual business, the consulting client for whom we created the leadership development process exemplifies this strategy. The system enabled a constant but flexible investment into the future of the company through continual improvement of its leaders, staff, and processes. You can apply the same approach to your own business or even your own career by developing a system that enables you to invest more efforts into improvements during good and calm times and scale down somewhat during busy or rough times.

Last but not least are two strategies: ***setting a policy to guide your future self and organization*** as well as ***making a precommitment.*** The two cofounders whose destructive conflicts threatened their company's future worked out a policy for their future selves that focused on the 99 percent of what unites them rather than the one percent that divides them. Moreover, they made a public commitment to each other of doing so and created a system to remind the other of these commitments in the heat of the moment.

The techniques in the last section of this chapter empower you and others in your organization and professional network to know what truly deserves your attention and what does not. In the next chapter, you'll get to combine everything you took from the chapters that detailed specific dangerous judgment errors and see how and where they show up in your workplace.

EXERCISE

Make sure you get the full benefit of paying attention to this chapter. Reflect on the following questions for a few minutes, and write down your answers in your professional journal:

- How will you use *considering alternative scenarios and options* to fight the biases described in this chapter? How will you help others in your organization and professional network use this strategy? What challenges do you anticipate in implementing this strategy and helping others do so, and what steps will you take to overcome these challenges?

- How will you use *probabilistic thinking* to fight the biases described in this chapter? How will you help others in your organization and professional network use this strategy? What challenges do you anticipate in implementing this strategy and helping others do so, and what steps will you take to overcome these challenges?

- How will you use *making predictions about the future* to fight the biases described in this chapter? How will you help others in your organization and professional network use this strategy? What challenges do you anticipate in implementing this strategy and helping others do so, and what steps will you take to overcome these challenges?

- How will you use *considering past experiences* to fight the biases described in this chapter? How will you help others in your organization and professional network use this strategy? What challenges do you anticipate in implementing this strategy and helping others do so, and what steps will you take to overcome these challenges?

- How will you use *considering the long-term future and repeating scenarios* to fight the biases described in this chapter? How will you help others in your organization and professional network use this strategy? What challenges do you anticipate in implementing this strategy and helping others do so, and what steps will you take to overcome these challenges?

✐ How will you use ***setting a policy to guide your future self and organization*** to fight the biases described in this chapter? How will you help others in your organization and professional network use this strategy? What challenges do you anticipate in implementing this strategy and helping others do so, and what steps will you take to overcome these challenges?

✐ How will you use ***making a precommitment*** to fight the biases described in this chapter? How will you help others in your organization and professional network use this strategy? What challenges do you anticipate in implementing this strategy and helping others do so, and what steps will you take to overcome these challenges?

CHAPTER SUMMARY

➡ Attention is the scarcest resource for business leaders, rather than money or time, yet we tend to underestimate the importance of this resource, and the fact that we can manipulate this resource effectively to achieve our business goals.

➡ When going with our gut, we pay too much attention to the most emotionally relevant factors in our immediate environment—the ones that feel like they are the most critical—whether or not they're the most important ones.

➡ Our intuition causes us to forget or deemphasize factors other than the ones right in front of our nose, meaning the ones to which we're paying attention in the moment.

➡ Our instinct is to focus excessively on the quantified measurements that we can see, as opposed to the actual outcomes that we want to achieve, which are often distinct from the measurements.

➡ We give short shrift to the future of our business activities, paying too much attention to short-term achievements at the expense of more important long-term ones.

➡ We underestimate the dangers of not taking actions.

➡ We tend to equate success with business competence, and ignore the role played by luck.

➡ Our gut reaction is to ignore important missing information, paying attention only to information that reaches us as opposed to looking for data that we should have but don't.

➡ Solving attention-related judgment errors requires us to use techniques that include:
>> considering alternative scenarios and options
>> probabilistic thinking
>> making predictions about the future
>> considering past experiences
>> considering the long-term future and repeating scenarios
>> setting a policy to guide your future self and organization
>> making a precommitment

Chapter 7

What Are the Dangerous Judgment Errors in Your Workplace?

Chapter Key Benefits

✿ Learn how to use a research-based assessment tool that identifies the prevalence of dangerous judgment errors in any workplace.

✿ Use this tool to identify the most common and impactful dangerous judgment errors for yourself and your organization.

✿ Decide on what specific judgment errors you and your team will work on next to protect yourself from business disasters.

So what kind of dangerous judgment errors are most prevalent in my business? Which of them bear the most threat for my bottom line? What should I tackle first, second, and third?

These are the most common questions asked in the latter parts of my keynotes and workshops after I describe the specific cognitive biases that carry the biggest risks for leaders and organizations, and relate a variety of strategies to address these problems. In other words, the audience grasps the content, and they are strongly motivated to defend themselves and their organizations from the devastating consequences of the problems I described. However, there's still a large gap between their emotional commitment to address cognitive biases and actually doing so. Namely, they don't know what the biggest dangers are and in what order they should tackle them; in other words, they're not confident about how to adapt this knowledge to their specific context.

At one point, the only option I had to offer involved hiring me as a consultant or coach to help them figure it out. However, given the limits of my time and the laws of supply and demand, many folks could not afford my services or needed help at a time when I and others from Disaster Avoidance Experts were committed to a different project. To address this challenge, I devised an assessment tool designed to help audience members answer their own questions called "Dangerous Judgment Errors in Your Workplace."

You are at that point in the book right now. By now, I hope you are inspired to protect your business and career from the systematic and predictable feelings and thinking errors we make as human beings. And because you did the exercises (right?) you're ahead of my audiences in regards to learning how dangerous judgment errors impact your business and career, and how you can apply the proven science-based strategies to address these problems.

This information will prove particularly valuable to you as you go through the assessment on the next pages. This tool will enable you to organize and categorize the information from the necessarily scattered exercises throughout the book and develop a plan of action for tackling cognitive biases to protect your bottom line.

Moreover, it will be helpful for others in your team and organization to take the assessment. Remember, just telling them about cognitive biases (according to extensive research on debiasing) will not be nearly enough to have them commit to these judgment errors. You need them to acknowledge where these biases lead to minor or major disasters in their workplace; the best strategy for doing so involves your team members diagnosing these problems independently of your direct input. One of the big strengths of the assessment is its orientation at the workplace as a whole, not the individual taking the assessment. This focus provides safety for individuals to diagnose problems caused by anyone—including themselves or others—without being blamed or admitting to personal faults.

There is an additional strength of the assessment: it asks the participant to attempt an evaluation of the financial impact of cognitive biases. Doing so will get your coworkers to recognize the bottom-line impact of such dangerous judgment errors. That impact on profits helps to convince them of the wisdom of taking steps to solve these problems. Fortunately, the assessment also provides guidance on how to decide and plan out these next steps.

In the first part of the assessment, you will evaluate how frequently each of these judgment errors occurs in your workplace. Next, you'll give your workplace a score based on your answers to reflect the prevalence of these cognitive biases. Then—because we are focusing on financial impact—you'll assess how much money they cost you, and decide how much you'd like to invest into addressing them. In the next section, you'll start transitioning to a more broad-picture approach that is needed to address these challenges by considering which of four key competencies in your organization is most threatened by judgment errors: evaluations of oneself, evaluations of others, strategic evaluations of risks and rewards, and tactical evaluations in project implementation. The final section provides specific directions for the next steps to resolve the systematic and predictable errors you've identified as most in need of addressing. To get a digital version of this assessment that you can share with your peers and colleagues, go to *www.DisasterAvoidanceExperts.com/NeverGut*.

Questionnaire

Each question refers to a problem that might occur in everyday professional situations. Your goal is to indicate how often the problem occurred in your workplace in the past year. The answer for each question will be in percentage terms out of all the possible times the problem might have occurred. If you are doing this assessment with a focus on a specific organizational department, team, or group, apply your evaluation only to that unit. Don't overthink it! Go with your initial impression, and don't try to be precise. If you feel something occurs infrequently, give it a low score; if you think it occurs frequently, give it a high score. Each question should take you *no more than fifteen to twenty seconds*. If it takes longer, you're overthinking. Take out your professional journal, and record your answers there, alongside all the other exercise answers.

#	Question
1	What percentage of projects missed the deadline or went over budget?
2	What percentage of team conflicts occurred because someone overestimated the effectiveness of their communication skills and persuasiveness?
3	Of all significant decisions, in what percentage of cases someone was overconfident about the decision?
4	Of all situations when someone had evidence that would contradict their beliefs (or clear information that would disprove their interpretation of the situation), in what percentage of cases did they ignore the evidence (or misinterpret the information)?
5	When an individual or a team had to deal with difficult and/or uncomfortable issues, in what percentage of situations did they focus on trivial issues instead?

#	Question
6	When a potential or current employee was evaluated, in what percentage of the situations was the evaluation too positive due to factors not relevant to their job competency or organizational fit?
7	When a potential or current employee was evaluated, in what percentage of the situations was the evaluation too negative due to factors not relevant to their job competency or organizational fit?
8	What percentage of team conflicts occurred because someone proposed ill considered or insufficiently thought out ideas?
9	What perecentage of team conflicts occurred because someone opposed innovative or surprising ideas?
10	Of all times when someone could have passed up the chain of command valuable but negative information, they failed to do so in what percentage of cases?
11	Of all times when someone defended an idea too strongly, in what percentage of cases did they come up with the idea?
12	In what percentage of cases did someone continue investing resources into an ongoing project, even though they had substantial evidence that the project was not succeeding?
13	Of all times when someone claimed that they had accurately predicted a specific development or outcome, in what percentage of cases did they actually not predict it?
14	Of all times when someone opposed making a change, in what percentage of cases did they did so only because it was a change, regardless of whether it would help the bottom line overall?

#	Question
15	Of all times when an inaccurate claim about something (a person, project, or other topic) became widely accepted, in what percentage of cases did this occur because the inaccurate claim was frequently repeated?
16	Of all times when there was an opportunity to take a worthwhile risk, in what percentage of situations was it not taken?
17	Of all times when someone claimed that they made no errors in judgment, in what percentage of times were they wrong?
18	Of all times when a disagreement occurred, in what percentage of times did someone let their desired conclusion influence their evaluation of the evidence?
19	Of all times when someone's behavior was attributed to their personality, in what percentage of cases was their behavior actually a result of the situation in which they found themselves?
20	What percentage of individual or team plans did not include contingencies for threats (or opportunities) that were unlikely to occur but could have significant consequences if they were to arise?
21	What percentage of individual or team plans overemphasized short-term and medium-term outcomes over long-term outcomes?
22	Of all times when someone claimed credit for themselves in a team project, in what percentage of cases did they claim more credit than they deserved?
23	Of all times when there was clear evidence of a problematic situation, in what percentage of cases did someone ignore it?

#	Question
24	Of all times when a decision was evaluated, in what percentage of times did someone focus mainly on the outcomes rather than consider the quality of the decision-making process?
25	Of all times when someone had to evaluate themselves, in what percentage of situations did they overestimate their positive qualities and underestimate their negative qualities?
26	Of all situations when an outcome was being measured, in what percentage of cases did someone conflate the means used to measure an outcome with the outcome itself (e.g., equate employee responses on satisfaction surveys with actual level of employee satisfaction)?
27	Of all situations when someone had all the relevant information needed to make a decision, in what percentage of cases did they continue to request additional information before making the decision?
28	Of all times when someone thought that others in the organization agreed with them, they were wrong in what percentage of cases?
29	Of all situations when an action was considered, in what percentage of cases were the costs of failing to act not adequately considered?
30	Of all times when someone was evaluating a situation and making a decision, in what percentage of cases did they underestimate the intensity of feelings of other people (employees, customers, vendors, or other stakeholders)?

Scoring Rubric

Add up all the answers to get the numerical score for your workplace. For the letter score, use the following guidelines to give your workplace a letter score. Treat the guidelines as an approximation, not as a conclusive determination.

For example, if the overall numerical score is 700, but four of the questions have a score of 90, this indicates that some areas of your workplace are experiencing high levels of dangerous judgment errors that need to be addressed. In that case, you should give your workplace a C as the letter score.

By contrast, if the score is 1,000 and all questions had a score of 30 or less, your workplace might need only minor tweaks to address dangerous judgment errors. These tweaks might include conducting some basic training on these errors and making some changes in your processes. In that case, you should give your workplace a B as the letter score.

Note that some judgment errors are much more dangerous than others. For instance, many strong companies suffered major setbacks when they inaccurately evaluated the intensity of feelings among stakeholders, such as the strength of customer loyalty or resistance to change among employees. Give your workplace a lower score if the identified judgment errors are particularly dangerous, based on your own estimate of the situation. Please make sure to provide a justification if your letter score differs from your numerical score.

0–300: A

Your workplace is experiencing a *minimal* level of dangerous judgment errors. Current processes and practices are working well and require normal vigilance for cognitive biases to protect your bottom line.

310–900: B

Your workplace is experiencing a *slight* level of dangerous judgment errors and requires some fine-tuning in current processes and practices to stop harming its bottom line.

910–1500: C

Your workplace is experiencing a *moderate* level of dangerous judgment errors and requires a substantial intervention to adjust current processes and practices to stop harming its bottom line.

1510–2100: D

Your workplace is experiencing a *high* level of dangerous judgment errors and requires major changes to current processes and practices in order to stop significant harm to its bottom line.

2110–3000: F

Your workplace is experiencing a *catastrophic* level of dangerous judgment errors and requires a full-scale overhaul of current processes and practices to stop harming its bottom line.

Write down your numerical score and then your letter score in your journal. If they differ, write down your justification for why they differ.

Impact Evaluation

This section provides a rough estimate of the financial impact of the judgment errors you uncovered and how much money you, your organization, department, or team will lose in the next year if the errors are not addressed.

Some of these errors are easy to quantify. For example, it's relatively easy to estimate the costs of missed deadlines, going over budget, or the costs of throwing good money thrown after bad. It's harder to assess the costs of judgment errors that result in issues like internal conflict or misinterpreted evidence. For these issues, you may choose to evaluate the financial consequences of the loss in productivity because of employee disengagement, time spent on internal politics over external productivity, and increased sick days due to a decrease in mental and physical well-being, as well as the losses that result from higher turnover and increased costs of hiring and training new employees.

✐ Write down your current annual revenue and expenses, to the extent that these are applicable to your role.

✐ Write down how much can you increase your revenue and decrease your expenses in the next year if you eliminate 20 percent of judgment errors in your workplace (20 percent is a conservative estimate of the impact of effective interventions as shown by behavioral science research).

✐ Given these numbers, write down how much you should invest into eliminating judgment errors.

Competencies

Dangerous judgment errors fall into four broad competencies: evaluations of oneself, evaluations of others, strategic evaluations of risks and rewards, and tactical evaluations in project implementation. Although these competencies overlap somewhat, we can generally place each question within one of these four competencies. Follow these steps to identify the competencies that are most affected by judgment errors in your workplace. Focus on improving performance in these areas for maximum impact.

Self-Evaluations

How good are the employees in your workplace at evaluating themselves?

Add your scores for the following questions:

Question	3	13	17	22	25	Total

Then, divide the total by 5. This percentage represents how frequently the employees in your workplace fall into judgment errors when evaluating themselves.

Anything over 10 percent is an issue. Anything over 30 percent is a problem. Anything over 50 percent is a serious problem.

OTHER EVALUATIONS

How good are your employees at evaluating others?

Add your scores for the following questions:

Question	2	6	7	10	19	28	30	Total

Divide the total by 7. This percentage represents how frequently the employees in your workplace fall into judgment errors when evaluating others.

Anything over 10 percent is an issue. Anything over 30 percent is a problem. Anything over 50 percent is a serious problem.

STRATEGIC EVALUATIONS

How good are the employees in your workplace at evaluating risks and rewards, making plans, and having foresight?

Add your scores for the following questions:

Question	4	5	8	9	11	14	15	16	1	20	23	Total

Divide the total by 11. This percentage represents how frequently the employees in your workplace fall into judgment errors when making strategic evaluations.

Anything over 10 percent is an issue. Anything over 30 percent is a problem. Anything over 50 percent is a serious problem.

TACTICAL EVALUATIONS

How good are the employees in your workplace at project development, implementation, and problem-solving?

Add your scores for the following questions:

Question	1	12	21	24	26	27	29	Total

Divide the total by 7. This percentage represents how frequently the employees in your workplace fall into judgment errors when making tactical evaluations.

Anything over 10 percent is an issue. Anything over 30 percent is a problem. Anything over 50 percent is a serious problem.

Next Steps: Address Judgment Errors

If your results suggest that some work is needed, the next step is to determine what areas require further work. Look over your answers from the assessment and focus on the ones you answered with 30 percent or higher. Prioritize a set of questions that require the most immediate work, next a set to work on in the short term, then a third set for the medium term, and delay action on the rest until later.

From my consulting and coaching experience, it's best to select no more than three questions per set if the questions are unrelated, although it's fine to select more if they are within a single competency. You can prioritize one of two ways: 1) based on the frequency of occurrence, namely, ones to which you gave a higher score, or 2) those having the most negative impact on your workplace, or other factors particular to your organization and your role. For example, you can focus on addressing a single competency if you are in a position to influence that competency most effectively. You can either determine these priorities by yourself or in collaboration with others (your colleagues, coach, consultant, or mentor).

Next, decide on how you'll work on these issues, using either in-house resources or tapping external resources. In either case, but especially if you use in-house resources, see the commentary on the following questions to help grasp the nature of and dangerous consequences of each judgment error to your workplace. Use this commentary to inform your work on the set of questions you chose, and refer back to the relevant section in the book that contains the specific case studies for each judgment error as well as the strategies best suited to address this problem.

QUESTION 1: What percentage of projects missed the deadline or went over budget?

This refers to the cognitive bias known as the *planning fallacy*, our tendency to assume that everything will go according to plan and consequently failing to build in needed resources to address the almost-inevitable problems that arise. In organizations, this tends to result in systematic cost and time overruns, which harm the bottom line through poor planning.

QUESTION 2: What percentage of team conflicts occurred because someone overestimated the effectiveness of their communication skills and persuasiveness?

This refers to the *illusion of transparency,* where we tend to overestimate how well other people understand how we feel and what we are trying to communicate, and overestimate how well we understand how other people feel and what they are trying to communicate to us. As a result, individuals make inaccurate assumptions about how other people will evaluate situations and make decisions, and these false assumptions lead to unneeded team conflict that decreases employee engagement and motivation, harms retention, and results in worse decisions.

QUESTION 3: Of all significant decisions, in what percentage of cases someone was overconfident about the decision?

This refers to *overconfidence bias,* our tendency to have excessively strong confidence in our evaluation of the situation. In organizational settings, overconfidence bias results in rushed decisions that have not been sufficiently examined. Such decisions hurt the bottom line because they fail to address threats or fail to take advantage of opportunities, either of which might have been recognized with additional information gathering before making the decision.

QUESTION 4: **Of all situations when someone had evidence that would contradict their beliefs (or clear information that would disprove their interpretation of the situation), in what percentage of cases did they ignore the evidence (or misinterpret the information)?**

This refers to the *confirmation bias,* which consists of two parts: a tendency to ignore information that goes against our preferred beliefs, and a tendency to look only for information that confirms our beliefs. The confirmation bias leads to the launch of pet projects that harm profitability and fail to address behaviors that lead to lawsuits, failure to give due consideration to suggestions that would substantially improve the bottom line, and other problems.

QUESTION 5: **When an individual or a team had to deal with difficult and/or uncomfortable issues, in what percentage of situations did they focus on trivial issues instead?**

This refers to the *Parkinson's law of triviality* or *bikeshedding,* which involves individuals or teams that focus on easy-to-address but comparatively trivial issues while they ignore difficult or uncomfortable issues that are much more important. For example, members of the marketing department spend their time on the nitty-gritty of website design while their overall advertising strategy is failing to bring potential customers to the website, or the sales department might debate the layout of the sales floor while the competition is increasingly outselling them.

QUESTION 6: **When a potential or current employee was evaluated, in what percentage of the situations was the evaluation too positive due to factors not relevant to their job competency or organizational fit?**

QUESTION 7: **When a potential or current employee was evaluated, in what percentage of the situations was the evaluation too negative due to factors not relevant to their job competency or organizational fit?**

These refer to a pair of judgment errors, the halo effect and the horns effect. The *halo effect* (question 6) refers to a tendency where if we like one characteristic of an individual that we consider important, we tend to rate all other characteristics of that individual as more positive than they really are. The **horns effect** (question 7) refers to the opposite tendency. These two biases are the bane of assessments and evaluations, whether for hiring or promotion, and have led to problems ranging from promotions for incompetent people while competent people are held back to serious lawsuits that crippled organizations and gravely tarnished their brands.

QUESTION 8: What percentage of team conflicts occurred because someone proposed ill considered or insufficiently thought out ideas?

QUESTION 9: What percentage of team conflicts occurred because someone opposed innovative or surprising ideas?

Questions 8 and 9 also refer to a pair of judgment errors, the **optimism bias** and the **pessimism bias.** The **optimism bias** (question 8) describes the many people who tend to make overly positive assessments of risks and rewards, while the **pessimism bias** (question 9) refers to those who make excessively negative assessments. Optimistically minded people are great at coming up with innovative new ideas without thinking through all the potential problems. By contrast, pessimistically inclined individuals come up with new ideas much less often because they tend to see all the potential problems in a magnified manner, and frequently criticize others who come up with new ideas because they can see all the risks that come with them. As a result, optimistic and pessimistic team members often have tension if they do not recognize and play to their strengths effectively.

QUESTION 10: Of all times when someone could have passed up the chain of command valuable but negative information, they failed to do so in what percentage of cases?

This refers to the **MUM effect** (also known as **shooting the messenger**), the tendency to blame the bearer of bad news for the bad news. This cognitive bias results in an organization's higher-level leaders failing to learn about the problems occurring at the grassroots level, with a resulting backlog of problems building up over time, thus damaging profitability and demoralizing employees.

QUESTION 11: Of all times when someone defended an idea too strongly, in what percentage of cases did they come up with the idea?

This refers to two related biases, the *IKEA effect* and *not invented here bias*. The *IKEA effect* refers to our tendency to overvalue our own ideas, products, and projects, while the *not invented here bias* describes an excessively negative evaluation of ideas, products, and projects that were not developed by us, our team, or our organization. Both of these tendencies are especially damaging for organizations that interact with the external environment, for instance when bringing products to market or when deciding whether to develop technologies internally or get them off the shelf.

QUESTION 12: In what percentage of cases did someone continue investing resources into an ongoing project, even though they had substantial evidence that the project was not succeeding?

This refers to the *sunk costs bias,* our tendency to continue to invest additional resources into projects, products, or relationships despite evidence that they are not working out. This tendency to throw good money after bad can be seen in companies that invest money into products or services that are not selling, who double down on a strategic direction when evidence suggests that it's going in the wrong direction, or stick with employees who should have been moved to a different position or let go much earlier.

QUESTION 13: Of all times when someone claimed that they had accurately predicted a specific development or outcome, in what percentage of cases did they actually not predict it?

This refers to the *hindsight bias,* our tendency to remember our evaluations and decisions as much more accurate than they actually were. In organizations, this tendency causes individuals to be excessively confident in their assessments in a way that undermines future decision-making and also leads to team conflicts when people disagree about the quality of past evaluations and decisions.

QUESTION 14: Of all times when someone opposed making a change, in what percentage of cases did they did so only because it was a change, regardless of whether it would help the bottom line overall?

This refers to the *status quo bias,* our tendency to prefer that things stay the same and to fear any changes. The status quo bias poses a high danger to organizations in our rapidly shifting world because it impedes their ability to adapt to changes quickly, as well as to forecast and adapt to changes.

QUESTION 15: Of all times when an inaccurate claim about something (a person, project, or other topic) became widely accepted, in what percentage of cases did this occur because the inaccurate claim was frequently repeated?

This refers to the *illusory truth effect,* our tendency to grow increasingly comfortable with statements that lack evidence and accept them as true just because they are frequently repeated. In an organizational context where certain individuals have control over trusted formal or informal channels of communication, said individuals can spread incorrect information for the sake of personal benefit and have it be accepted as true through mere repetition while harming the organization's ability to make wise decisions.

QUESTION 16: Of all times when there was an opportunity to take a worthwhile risk, in what percentage of situations was it not taken?

This refers to *loss aversion,* our tendency to avoid risking small losses at the cost of substantially larger gains. The result in organizations is a tendency to play it safe in lieu of taking smart risks, thus harming profitability.

QUESTION 17: Of all times when someone claimed that they made no errors in judgment, in what percentage of times were they wrong?

This refers to *bias blind spot,* our tendency to believe that we have no blind spots and have a perfectly clear vision of reality and that our decision-making is optimal, even though our vision is clouded by dozens of cognitive biases. The result of this bias in organizations is arrogance. As the saying goes, "Pride goeth before a fall."

Question 18: Of all times when a disagreement occurred, in what percentage of times did someone let their desired conclusion influence their evaluation of the evidence?

This refers to *belief bias,* the tendency to permit our personal beliefs and preferences to sway our perception and interpretation of evidence, especially when making decisions. As a consequence of belief bias, decisions in organizations are made based on the personal likes and dislikes of leaders rather than the quality of evidence, inevitably undermining the company's bottom line.

Question 19: Of all times when someone's behavior was attributed to their personality, in what percentage of cases was their behavior actually a result of the situation in which they found themselves?

This refers to the *fundamental attribution error,* our tendency to attribute negative behaviors to the personality of other people rather than the context. Such incorrect attribution can gravely damage relationships within an organization or with external stakeholders, with the former undercutting employee motivation and engagement, and the latter harming reputation and external collaborations.

Question 20: What percentage of individual or team plans did not include contingencies for threats (or opportunities) that were unlikely to occur but could have significant consequences if they were to arise?

This refers to the *normalcy bias,* our tendency to ignore predictable major threats that did not happen previously. Thus, organizations might not pay proper attention to the need to protect themselves against potential disasters despite having more than sufficient information about a major threat, with devastating consequences when these disasters happen to them. The same applies to organizations that fail to prepare themselves to take advantage of outstanding opportunities.

QUESTION 21: What percentage of individual or team plans over-emphasized short-term and medium-term outcomes over long-term outcomes?

This refers to *hyperbolic discounting,* our tendency to prefer immediate gains over larger rewards later, even if the latter would be more beneficial in the long term. An orientation toward such short-term rewards in organizations, usually caused by problematic incentive structures for performance evaluation or external market pressure from investors, undermines long-term profitability.

QUESTION 22: Of all times when someone claimed credit for themselves in a team project, in what percentage of cases did they claim more credit than they deserved?

This refers to *egocentric bias,* our tendency to claim more credit for ourselves from successful joint projects than is accurate, and vice versa for failed projects. This tendency damages relationships within teams and exacerbates internal organizational politics, undercutting employee engagement, motivation, and retention.

QUESTION 23: Of all times when there was clear evidence of a problematic situation, in what percentage of cases did someone ignore it?

This refers to the *ostrich effect,* our tendency to deny clear negative facts. A study found that of all CEOs fired, more than 20 percent are dismissed for failing to acknowledge negative information about an organization's performance. This tendency impacts people at all levels of the organization. Such failure results in further deterioration of performance and needed organizational changes are not brought about.

QUESTION 24: Of all times when a decision was evaluated, in what percentage of times did someone focus mainly on the outcomes rather than consider the quality of the decision-making process?

This refers to the *outcome bias,* our tendency to evaluate decisions by their outcome rather than the quality of the process by which decisions were made. Even broken clocks are right twice a day, and failing to evaluate the process results in the highly problematic tendency of rewards, such as promotions going to the lucky as opposed to the good. Of course, luck runs out while quality persists; it's much more beneficial for an organization to reward and promote those who are good even when they are unlucky.

QUESTION 25: Of all times when someone had to evaluate themselves, in what percentage of situations did they overestimate their positive qualities and underestimate their negative qualities?

This refers to *illusory superiority,* our tendency to evaluate our positive qualities as better than they are, and dismiss our negative qualities. This tendency results in unnecessary team conflicts and internal politics.

QUESTION 26: Of all situations when an outcome was being measured, in what percentage of cases did someone conflate the means used to measure an outcome with the outcome itself (e.g., equate employee responses on satisfaction surveys with actual level of employee satisfaction)?

This refers to *surrogation,* our tendency to lose sight of the outcome that a specific measuring technique is supposed to evaluate, thus conflating the measure with the outcome. In an organization, the danger comes when those in leadership positions mistakenly equate the various reports and statistics they receive to what those reports and statistics are supposed to measure. For instance, a report on customer satisfaction does not equate to actual customer satisfaction; the report is only as good as the data that went into the report, combined with the biases of those who prepared the report. This is especially problematic in larger organizations where the leadership is further away from the front lines. In these cases, surrogation causes the leadership to try to improve the measure rather than the outcome—what gets measured gets managed—harming the organization's performance and profitability.

QUESTION 27: Of all situations when someone had all the relevant information needed to make a decision, in what percentage of cases did they continue to request additional information before making the decision?

This refers to the *information bias,* our tendency to seek more information than is needed to make decisions and take action. Organizations where information bias is common are characterized by analysis paralysis, that is, not taking actions and making decisions quickly enough, and as a result failing to compete effectively in the marketplace.

QUESTION 28: Of all times when someone thought that others in the organization agreed with them, they were wrong in what percentage of cases?

This refers to the *false consensus effect,* our tendency to overestimate the extent to which other people share our beliefs, preferences, and conclusions, also known as *typical mind fallacy.* This tendency causes significant internal team conflict when these disagreements become apparent as the rubber hits the road on projects and decisions, and undermines employee motivation, engagement, and retention. It also causes organizations to make products and offer services that do not satisfy customer needs because they are making unwarranted assumptions about how well they know their customers.

QUESTION 29: Of all situations when an action was considered, in what percentage of cases were the costs of failing to act not adequately considered?

This refers to the *omission bias,* our tendency to judge harmful action as worse than harmful inactions (omissions to act). Harmful inactions—whether failing to address threats or take advantage of opportunities—are just as damaging to an organization's bottom line, reputation, and other assets, as are harmful actions, and need to be treated the same.

QUESTION 30: Of all times when someone was evaluating a situation and making a decision, in what percentage of cases did they underestimate the intensity of feelings of other people (employees, customers, vendors, or other stakeholders)?

This refers to the *empathy gap,* our tendency to underestimate the intensity of feelings of people with whom we disagree or whom we do not see as belonging to the same group as we do. The empathy gap is one of the most insidious biases for organizations, as its occurrence is often hard to recognize; it becomes apparent only when new internal changes or external offerings are met with great resistance, to the utter surprise of those behind the changes or offerings.

CHAPTER SUMMARY

☛ The "Dangerous Judgment Errors in Your Workplace" assessment has five functions:

» Adapt the cutting-edge research on dangerous judgment errors to your specific context.

» Identify the most common and problematic cognitive biases in your workplace.

» Inform your team members who take the assessment about such dangerous judgment errors in a persuasive manner that encourages them to avoid these errors.

» Assess the financial impact of these cognitive biases as the first step to address these problems.

» Decide which specific dangerous judgment errors to target first, and plan specific next steps to tackle these errors.

Conclusion

Many high-flying professionals, including business leaders at the very top, shrink away from learning about dangerous judgment errors because doing so can be hard and unpleasant. It's counterintuitive and takes them outside their comfort zone of going with their gut. It goes against the typical structures and incentives in teams and organizations that usually favor trusting intuition and being authentic.

Moreover, many (not all) of the most successful leaders and professionals believe they are perfect decision-makers. After all, they have succeeded so far!

Unfortunately, the greatest disasters happen to those who have been most successful, usually because they continue to use methods that worked for them in the past in new contexts where their previous methods no longer apply. They also get cut off from previous trusted sources of key information as they advance in their careers, which results in more and more distortions, and in turn, results in worse and worse judgments. This tendency helps explain this book's many examples of highly competent and successful business leaders who steered their companies and careers into destruction.

Having read this book, you're in a vastly privileged position compared to these business leaders and any other professionals who are unaware of the dangers of typical judgment errors in the workplace. The thirty cognitive biases described here represent the biggest threats to your business and career success. Let me repeat: the biggest threats.

From the extensive research cited in this book—as well as my clients' case studies—you know that the external context represents a much lesser danger to businesses than poor decisions in strategic direction, in business relationships, and in project implementation.

If you and your organization can avoid even a fraction of the dangerous judgment errors we suffer because we're adapted for the ancient savanna and not the modern businesses environment, you set yourself on the path to success.

To do so, make sure to spread the paradigm shift in this book to your team and those in your professional contact network who you don't want to see suffer from business disasters. My personal code of ethics—minimizing suffering and improving well-being—impels me to spread this message as widely as possible. I invite you to join me in doing so for those whose success you care about. You'll find that some are resistant at first because of the unfortunate advice from prominent business gurus who encourage their followers to trust their guts. Keep at it, and demonstrate why savanna-adapted intuitions are a horrible guide for the modern business environment. They will thank you for your persistence.

Let me be clear: like a broken clock that's right twice a day, it doesn't mean that your or their gut is never right. It's simply the case that you should never go with your gut because of the overwhelming number of scenarios in which it misfires in the current business environment. If you feel discomfort with a situation, don't just rely on your instincts and go with your autopilot system. Instead, turn on the intentional system to analyze what's going on. Evaluate whether you are impacted by any of the thirty cognitive biases, and use one or more of the debiasing strategies to address the potential for judgment errors.

It's hard to keep all of the thirty judgment errors in mind without extensive practice, and I struggled to do so when learning about them. Keep the book close by to review these cognitive biases and the specific strategies most useful in addressing them. At regular intervals, such as once a quarter, review your answers to the exercises, which I'm sure you did in order to defend yourself from suffering the disasters of failing to integrate these strategies. Update your answers based on your experiences that quarter.

It's easy to read this book. The harder thing to do is the challenging reflection required to protect yourself and your business from judgment errors. It is even more difficult to integrate what you realized into your day-to-day work.

So what kind of story do you want to tell about yourself three months from now? Do you want to be the person that read a paradigm-shifting book but work got away from you and you let these strategies slip away, suffering the disasters that followed? Alternatively, do you want to tell the story that you read a paradigm-shifting book, did all the exercises to adapt the new information into your professional context, and invested the efforts to integrate these strategies into your work to take your and your team's performance to the next level and leave the competition in the dust?

Which of these stories reflects the kind of leader you want to be and the future in which you want to live? The choice is yours.

If you're the second type of leader, I can promise that you'll achieve the three commitments I made at the beginning of this book. First, you'll stand head and shoulders above the competition when you defend yourself from numerous potential threats and are optimally prepared to take advantage of unexpected opportunities, thus maximizing your bottom line. Second, you can feel safe and confident, sleeping soundly at night knowing that by avoiding dangerous judgment, you will automatically exceed expectations for your clients, colleagues, vendors, investors, and any other internal and external stakeholders. Third, you'll have much less frustration, stress, and anxiety in your day-to-day work because of your ability to have outstanding business relationships inside and outside your organization. Those to whom you spread this information will get similar benefits.

The eight-step decision-making model provides much-needed guidance for pulling together and implementing the debiasing strategies in this book when the rubber meets the road:

1. Identify the need for a decision to be made.

2. Gather relevant information from a variety of informed perspectives on the issue at hand.

3. Decide on the goals you want to reach, and paint a clear vision of the desired outcome.

4. Develop clear decision-making criteria to evaluate options.

5. Generate viable options that can achieve your goals.

6. Weigh these options and pick the best of the bunch.

7. Implement the option you chose.

8. Evaluate the implementation process and revise as needed.

Using these steps for any significant decision—either one-time decisions with a substantial impact or a series of repeating decisions—will automatically address most cognitive biases.

Make sure to ask the five key questions to avoid decision disasters as you go through all of these steps:

1. What important info didn't I yet fully consider?
2. What relevant dangerous judgment errors didn't I yet address?
3. What would a trusted and objective adviser suggest I do?
4. How have I addressed all the ways it could fail?
5. What new info would cause me to revisit the decision?

Ask these questions especially when you are under intense pressure to make decisions quickly and don't have the chance to go through each of the eight steps thoroughly.

When you integrate the eight-step decision-making model and the five questions as key processes, not simply for yourself, but also for your team and organization as a whole, you will maximize your chances of besting your competition and bringing the most value to your customers and investors. For more than twenty years, my consulting and coaching clients, ranging from Fortune 500 companies to midsize businesses and nonprofits, have benefited greatly from these and other strategies described in this book. Now, you can do so as well.

You can find many more resources adapted to business needs at *www.DisasterAvoidanceExperts.com/NeverGut*. For bulk discounts, write to *Info@DisasterAvoidanceExperts.com*. I'm eager to hear your questions at *Gleb@DisasterAvoidanceExperts.com*.

The most important—and most challenging—takeaway is: ***What feels comfortable is often exactly the wrong thing for our bottom line***. In our technologically disrupted environment, the future is never going to be like today. We have to adapt constantly to an increasingly changing environment to ensure the success of our business and our careers. That ever-intensifying pace of change means our gut reactions will be less and less suited in the future, and relying on our autopilot system will lead us to crash and burn.

The ones who survive and flourish in the world of tomorrow will recognize this paradigm shift. They will adopt counterintuitive, uncomfortable, and highly profitable techniques to avoid business disasters, and make the best decisions by relying on their intentional system to address the systematic and predictable errors we all tend to make. It is my fervent hope that you join them and minimize suffering and maximize well-being for you, your team, and everyone with whom you share this paradigm shift. To your good judgment, my friends!

Notes

Introduction

1. Emily Pronin, Daniel Y. Lin, and Lee Ross. "The bias blind spot: Perceptions of bias in self versus others." *Personality and Social Psychology Bulletin* 28, no.3 (2002): 369–381.

2. Paul Carroll and Chunka Mui. *Billion Dollar Lessons: What You Can Learn from the Most Inexcusable Business Failures of the Last Twenty-five Years.* New York: Penguin, 2008.

3. "Do economic or industry factors affect business survival?" *SBA Office of Advocacy.* June 2012. *www.sba.gov*

Chapter 1

1. "Equifax data breach was 'entirely preventable,' congressional report finds." *CBS News,* Dec. 11, 2018, *www.cbsnews.com*

2. Sarah Whitten, Betsy Spring, and Kate Rogers. "Papa John's founder John Schnatter finally has his day in court, testifies against the board." *CNBC.* Oct. 1, 2018, *www.cnbc.com*

3. Michael Liedtke. "Musk out as Tesla chair, remains CEO in $40M SEC settlement." *AP News,* Sept. 30, 2018, *https://apnews.com*

4. Mark Murphy. "Leadership IQ study: Mismanagement, inaction among the real reasons why CEOs get fired." Oct. 26, 2018, *www.prweb.com*

5. Richard S. Tedlow. *Denial: Why Business Leaders Fail to Look Facts in the Face—and What to Do About It.* New York: Penguin, 2010.

6. Sigmund Freud. *The Ego and the Id.* No. 142. New York: W. W. Norton & Company, 1923.

7. Daniel Kahneman. *Thinking, Fast and Slow.* New York: Farrar, Straus and Giroux, 2011.

8. Marco Del Giudice. *Evolutionary Psychopathology: A Unified Approach.* Oxford, UK: Oxford University Press, 2018.

9. Joy F. Baumeister and John Tierney. *Willpower: Rediscovering the Greatest Human Strength.* New York: Penguin, 2012; Veronika Job, Carol S. Dweck, and Gregory M. Walton. "Ego depletion—Is it all in your head? Implicit theories about willpower affect self-regulation." *Psychological Science* 21, no. 11 (2010): 1686–1693.

10. Gerd Gigerenzer. *Gut Feelings: The Intelligence of the Unconscious.* New York: Penguin, 2007; Gerd Gigerenzer and Reinhard Selten, eds. *Bounded Rationality: The Adaptive Toolbox.* Cambridge, MA: MIT Press, 2002.

11. Charles F. Bond Jr. and Bella M. DePaulo. "Accuracy of deception judgments." *Personality and Social Psychology Review* 10, no. 3 (2006): 214–234.

12. Dan Ariely. *Predictably Irrational.* New York: HarperCollins, 2008; Mahzarin R. Banaji and Anthony G. Greenwald. *Blindspot: Hidden Biases of Good People.* New York: Delacorte Press, 2013.

13. Balazs Aczel, Bence Bago, Aba Szollosi, Andrei Foldes, and Bence Lukacs. "Is it time for studying real-life debiasing? Evaluation of the effectiveness of an analogical intervention technique." *Frontiers in Psychology* 6 (2015): 1–13; Sammy Almashat, Brian Ayotte, Barry Edelstein, and Jennifer Margrett. "Framing effect debiasing in medical decision making." *Patient Education and Counseling* 71, no. 1 (2008): 102–107; Craig A. Anderson. "Inoculation and counterexplanation: Debiasing techniques in the perseverance of social theories." *Social Cognition* 1, no. 2 (1982): 126–139; Hal R. Arkes. "Costs and benefits

of judgment errors: Implications for debiasing." *Psychological Bulletin* 110, no. 3 (1991): 486–498; Jonathan Baron. *Thinking and Deciding.* Cambridge, UK: Cambridge University Press, 2000; Jonathan Baron, Jane Beattie, and John C. Hershey. "Heuristics and biases in diagnostic reasoning: II. Congruence, information, and certainty." *Organizational Behavior and Human Decision Processes* 42, no. 1 (1988): 88–110; Guillaume Beaulac and Tim Kenyon. "Critical thinking education and debiasing (AILACT Essay Prize Winner 2013)." *Informal Logic* 34, no. 4 (2014): 341–363; Izak Benbasat and John Lim. "Information technology support for debiasing group judgments: An empirical evaluation." *Organizational Behavior and Human Decision Processes* 83, no. 1 (2000): 167–183; Bret G. Bentz, Donald A. Williamson, and Susan F. Franks. "Debiasing of pessimistic judgments associated with anxiety." *Journal of Psychopathology and Behavioral Assessment* 26, no. 3 (2004): 173–180; Gokul Bhandari, Khaled Hassanein, and Richard Deaves. "Debiasing investors with decision support systems: An experimental investigation." *Decision Support Systems* 46, no. 1 (2008): 399–410; Kemal B. Büyükkurt and Meral Demirbag Büyükkurt. "An experimental study of the effectiveness of three debiasing techniques." *Decision Sciences* 22, no. 1 (1991): 60–73; Fei-Fei Cheng and Chin-Shan Wu. "Debiasing the framing effect: The effect of warning and involvement." *Decision Support Systems* 49, no. 3 (2010): 328–334; Peter M. Clarkson, Craig Emby, and Vanessa W-S. Watt. "Debiasing the outcome effect: The role of instructions in an audit litigation setting." *Auditing: A Journal of Practice & Theory* 21, no. 2 (2002): 7–20; Robert T. Clemen and Kenneth C. Lichtendahl. "Debiasing expert overconfidence: A Bayesian calibration model." In *Sixth International Conference on Probablistic Safety Assessment and Management* (2002): 1–16; Pat Croskerry. "Cognitive forcing strategies in clinical decision-making." *Annals of Emergency Medicine* 41, no. 1 (2003): 110–120; Pat Croskerry. "When I say...cognitive debiasing." *Medical Education* 49, no. 7 (2015): 656–657; Pat Croskerry, Geeta Singhal, and Sílvia Mamede. "Cognitive debiasing 1: Origins of bias and theory of debiasing." *BMJ Qual Saf* (2013): 1–7; Daniel Dennett. "Intentional systems theory." *The Oxford Handbook of Philosophy of Mind* (2009): 339–350; Rolf Dobelli. *The Art of Thinking Clearly: Better Thinking, Better Decisions.* London: Hachette UK, 2013; J. St

BT Evans, S. E. Newstead, J. L. Allen, and P. Pollard. "Debiasing by instruction: The case of belief bias." *European Journal of Cognitive Psychology* 6, no. 3 (1994): 263–285; Bent Flyvbjerg. "Curbing optimism bias and strategic misrepresentation in planning: Reference class forecasting in practice." *European Planning Studies* 16, no. 1 (2008): 3–21; Cary Frydman and Antonio Rangel. "Debiasing the disposition effect by reducing the saliency of information about a stock's purchase price." *Journal of Economic Behavior & Organization* 107 (2014): 541–552; Adam Daniel Galinsky. "Perspective-taking: Debiasing social thought (stereotyping)." *ProQuest Information & Learning* (1999): 708–724; Atul Gawande. *The Checklist Manifesto: How to Get Things Right.* New York: Henry Holt and Company, 2009; Paul Goodwin and Richard Lawton. "Debiasing forecasts: How useful is the unbiasedness test?" *International Journal of Forecasting* 19, no. 3 (2003): 467–475; Lorenz Graf, Andreas König, Albrecht Enders, and Harald Hungenberg. "Debiasing competitive irrationality: How managers can be prevented from trading off absolute for relative profit." *European Management Journal* 30, no. 4 (2012): 386–403; Andrew C. Hafenbrack, Zoe Kinias, and Sigal G. Barsade. "Debiasing the mind through meditation: Mindfulness and the sunk-cost bias." *Psychological Science* 25, no. 2 (2014): 369–376; Jonathan Haidt. *The Happiness Hypothesis: Putting Ancient Wisdom and Philosophy to the Test of Modern Science.* London: Arrow, 2007; Chip Heath and Dan Heath. *Decisive: How to Make Better Choices in Life and at Work.* New York: Random House, 2013; Chip Heath and Dan Heath. *Switch: How to Change When Change Is Hard.* New York: Crown Business, 2010; Edward R. Hirt, Frank R. Kardes, and Keith D. Markman. "Activating a mental simulation mind-set through generation of alternatives: Implications for debiasing in related and unrelated domains." *Journal of Experimental Social Psychology* 40, no. 3 (2004): 374–383; Edward R. Hirt and Keith D. Markman. "Multiple explanation: A consider-an-alternative strategy for debiasing judgments." *Journal of Personality and Social Psychology* 69, no. 6 (1995): 1069–1086; Barbara E. Kahn, Mary Frances Luce, and Stephen M. Nowlis. "Debiasing insights from process tests." *Journal of Consumer Research* 33, no. 1 (2006): 131–138; Frank R. Kardes, Steven S. Posavac, David Silvera, Maria L. Cronley, David M. Sanbonmatsu, Susan Schertzer, Felicia Miller, Paul

M. Herr, and Murali Chandrashekaran. "Debiasing omission neglect." *Journal of Business Research* 59, no. 6 (2006): 786–792; Markku Kaustia and Milla Perttula. "Overconfidence and debiasing in the financial industry." *Review of Behavioural Finance* 4, no. 1 (2012): 46–62; Gideon Keren. "Cognitive aids and debiasing methods: can cognitive pills cure cognitive ills?." In *Advances in Psychology*, vol. 68 (1990): 523–552; Tim Kenyon. "False polarization: debiasing as applied social epistemology." *Synthese* 191, no. 11 (2014): 2529–2547; Laura J. Kray and Adam D. Galinsky. "The debiasing effect of counterfactual mind-sets: Increasing the search for disconfirmatory information in group decisions." *Organizational Behavior and Human Decision Processes* 91, no. 1 (2003): 69–81; Justin Kruger and Matt Evans. "If you don't want to be late, enumerate: Unpacking reduces the planning fallacy." *Journal of Experimental Social Psychology* 40, no. 5 (2004): 586–598; Richard P. Larrick. "Debiasing." *Blackwell Handbook of Judgment and Decision Making* (2004): 316–338; Stephan Lewandowsky, Ullrich KH Ecker, Colleen M. Seifert, Norbert Schwarz, and John Cook. "Misinformation and its correction: Continued influence and successful debiasing." *Psychological Science in the Public Interest* 13, no. 3 (2012): 106–131; Scott O. Lilienfeld, Rachel Ammirati, and Kristin Landfield. "Giving debiasing away: Can psychological research on correcting cognitive errors promote human welfare?" *Perspectives on Psychological Science* 4, no. 4 (2009): 390–398; Lai-Huat Lim and Izak Benbasat. "The debiasing role of group support systems: An experimental investigation of the representativeness bias." *International Journal of Human-Computer Studies* 47, no. 3 (1997): 453–471; Lola L. Lopes. "Procedural debiasing." *Acta Psychologica* 64, no. 2 (1987): 167–185; Donald L. McCabe and Linda Klebe Trevino. "Academic dishonesty: Honor codes and other contextual influences." *The Journal of Higher Education* 64, no. 5 (1993): 522–538; Donald L. McCabe, Linda Klebe Trevino, and Kenneth D. Butterfield. "Academic integrity in honor code and non-honor code environments: A qualitative investigation." *The Journal of Higher Education* 70, no. 2 (1999): 211–234; David McRaney. *You Are Not So Smart: Why You Have Too Many Friends on Facebook, Why Your Memory Is Mostly Fiction, and 46 Other Ways You're Deluding Yourself.* Gotham Books/Penguin Group, 2011; Alfred R. Mele. *Irrationality: An Essay on Akrasia, Self-Deception, and Self-*

Control. Oxford: Oxford University Press on Demand, 1992; Audrey K. Miller, Keith D. Markman, Maverick M. Wagner, and Amy N. Hunt. "Mental simulation and sexual prejudice reduction: The debiasing role of counterfactual thinking." *Journal of Applied Social Psychology* 43, no. 1 (2013): 190–194; Carey K. Morewedge, Haewon Yoon, Irene Scopelliti, Carl W. Symborski, James H. Korris, and Karim S. Kassam. "Debiasing decisions: Improved decision making with a single training intervention." *Policy Insights from the Behavioral and Brain Sciences* 2, no. 1 (2015): 129–140; Bhagwant N. Persaud and Ezra Hauer. "Comparison of two methods for debiasing before-and-after accident studies." *Transportation Research Record* 975 (1984): 1 Persaud, 7; Michael A. Roberto. *Know What You Don't Know: How Great Leaders Prevent Problems Before They Happen.* New Jersey: Pearson Prentice Hall, 2009; Jason R. Rose. "Debiasing comparative optimism and increasing worry for health outcomes." *Journal of Health Psychology* 17, no. 8 (2012): 1121–1131; Lee Ross and Richard E. Nisbett. *The Person and the Situation: Perspectives of Social Psychology.* Brixton, UK: Pinter & Martin Publishers, 2011; Lawrence J. Sanna, Norbert Schwarz, and Shevaun L. Stocker. "When debiasing backfires: Accessible content and accessibility experiences in debiasing hindsight." *Journal of Experimental Psychology: Learning, Memory, and Cognition* 28, no. 3 (2002): 497–502; Thomas C. Schelling. *The Strategy of Conflict.* Cambridge, MA: Harvard University Press, 1960; Alison C. Smith and Edith Greene. "Conduct and its consequences: Attempts at debiasing jury judgments." *Law and Human Behavior* 29, no. 5 (2005): 505–526; Keither Stanovich. *Rationality and the Reflective Mind.* Oxford, UK: Oxford University Press, 2011; Cass R. Sunstein and Christine Jolls. "Debiasing Through Law" (John M. Olin *Program in Law and Economics Working Paper* No. 225 (2004): 1–53; Philip E. Tetlock. "Accountability: A social check on the fundamental attribution error." *Social Psychology Quarterly* (1985): 227–236; Philip E. Tetlock. *Expert Political Judgment: How Good Is It? How Can We Know?* Princeton, NJ: Princeton University Press, 2017; Philip E. Tetlock and Dan Gardner. *Superforecasting: The Art and Science of Prediction.* New York: Random House, 2016; Philip E. Tetlock, Gregory Mitchell, and Terry L. Murray. "The challenge of debiasing personnel decisions: Avoiding both under- and overcorrection." *Industrial and*

Organizational Psychology 1, no. 4 (2008): 439–443; Richard H. Thaler. *Nudge: Improving Decisions About Health, Wealth, and Happiness.* New Haven, CT: Yale University Press, 2008; Gleb Tsipursky. *The Truth-Seeker's Handbook: A Science-Based Guide.* Columbus, OH: Intentional Insights, 2017; Gleb Tsipursky and Fabio Votta. "Fighting fake news and post-truth politics with behavioral science: The pro-truth pledge." *Behavior and Social Issues* 27, no. 2 (2018): 47–70; Gleb Tsipursky, Fabio Votta, and James Mulick. "Fighting fake news with psychology. The pro-truth pledge." *Journal of Social and Political Psychology* 6, no. 2 (2018): 271–290; Gleb Tsipursky and Zachary Morford. "Addressing behaviors that lead to sharing fake news." *Behavior and Social Issues* 27 (2018): 6–10; Michael Vaughan. *The Thinking Effect: Rethinking Thinking to Create Great Leaders and the New Value Worker.* London: Hachette UK, 2013; Neil D. Weinstein and William M. Klein. "Resistance of personal risk perceptions to debiasing interventions." *Health Psychology* 14, no. 2 (1995): 132–140.

Chapter 2

1. Mohammed Abdellaoui, Han Bleichrodt, and Corina Paraschiv. "Loss aversion under prospect theory: A parameter-free measurement." *Management Science* 53, no. 10 (2007): 1659–1674; Shlomo Benartzi and Richard H. Thaler. "Myopic loss aversion and the equity premium puzzle." *The Quarterly Journal of Economics* 110, no. 1 (1995): 73–92; David Bowman, Deborah Minehart, and Matthew Rabin. "Loss aversion in a consumption–savings model." *Journal of Economic Behavior & Organization* 38, no. 2 (1999): 155–178; Colin Camerer. "Three cheers—psychological, theoretical, empirical—for loss aversion." *Journal of Marketing Research* 42, no. 2 (2005): 129–133; James J. Chrisman and Pankaj C. Patel. "Variations in R&D investments of family and nonfamily firms: Behavioral agency and myopic loss aversion perspectives." *Academy of Management Journal* 55, no. 4 (2012): 976–997; David Genesove and Christopher Mayer. "Loss aversion and seller behavior: Evidence from the housing market." *The Quarterly Journal of Economics* 116, no. 4 (2001): 1233–1260; Michael S. Haigh and John A. List. "Do professional traders exhibit myopic loss

aversion? An experimental analysis." *The Journal of Finance* 60, no. 1 (2005): 523–534; Deborah A. Kermer, Erin Driver-Linn, Timothy D. Wilson, and Daniel T. Gilbert. "Loss aversion is an affective forecasting error." *Psychological Science* 17, no. 8 (2006): 649–653; Veronika Köbberling and Peter Wakker. "An index of loss aversion." *Journal of Economic Theory* (2005): 119–131; Nathan Novemsky and Daniel Kahneman. "The boundaries of loss aversion." *Journal of Marketing research* 42, no. 2 (2005): 119–128; Richard H. Thaler, Amos Tversky, Daniel Kahneman, and Alan Schwartz. "The effect of myopia and loss aversion on risk taking: An experimental test." *The Quarterly Journal of Economics* 112, no. 2 (1997): 647–661; Sabrina M. Tom, Craig R. Fox, Christopher Trepel, and Russell A. Poldrack. "The neural basis of loss aversion in decision-making under risk." *Science* 315, no. 5811 (2007): 515–518; Amos Tversky and Daniel Kahneman. "Loss aversion in riskless choice: A reference-dependent model." *The Quarterly Journal of Economics* 106, no. 4 (1991): 1039–1061.

2. Katrin Burmeister and Christian Schade. "Are entrepreneurs' decisions more biased? An experimental investigation of the susceptibility to status quo bias." *Journal of Business Venturing* 22, no. 3 (2007): 340–362; Raquel Fernandez and Dani Rodrik. "Resistance to reform: Status quo bias in the presence of individual-specific uncertainty." *The American Economic Review* (1991): 1146–1155; Yusufcan Masatlioglu and Efe A. Ok. "Rational choice with status quo bias." *Journal of Economic Theory* 121, no. 1 (2005): 1–29; William Samuelson and Richard Zeckhauser. "Status quo bias in decision making." *Journal of Risk and Uncertainty* 1, no. 1 (1988): 7–59.

3. Michael Thompson and Aaron Wildavsky. "A cultural theory of information bias in organizations." *Journal of Management Studies* 23, no. 3 (1986): 273–286; Lyn M. Van Swol. "Perceived importance of information: The effects of mentioning information, shared information bias, ownership bias, reiteration, and confirmation bias." *Group Processes & Intergroup Relations* 10, no. 2 (2007): 239–256.

4. Howard Garland and Stephanie Newport. "Effects of absolute and relative sunk costs on the decision to persist with a course of action." *Organizational Behavior and Human Decision Processes* 48, no. 1 (1991):

55–69; Gregory B. Northcraft and Gerrit Wolf. "Dollars, sense, and sunk costs: A life cycle model of resource allocation decisions." *Academy of Management Review* 9, no. 2 (1984): 225–234; Jonathan O'Brien and Timothy Folta. "Sunk costs, uncertainty and market exit: A real options perspective." *Industrial and Corporate Change* 18, no. 5 (2009): 807–833; Filip Roodhooft and Luk Warlop. "On the role of sunk costs and asset specificity in outsourcing decisions: A research note." *Accounting, Organizations and Society* 24, no. 4 (1999): 363–369.

5. Robert Franciosi, Praveen Kujal, Roland Michelitsch, Vernon Smith, and Gang Deng. "Experimental tests of the endowment effect." *Journal of Economic Behavior & Organization* 30, no. 2 (1996): 213–226; Jochen Reb and Terry Connolly. "Possession, feelings of ownership, and the endowment effect." *Judgment and Decision Making* 2, no. 2 (2007): 107–114; Daniel Kahneman, Jack L. Knetsch, and Richard H. Thaler. "Anomalies: The endowment effect, loss aversion, and status quo bias." *Journal of Economic Perspectives* 5, no. 1 (1991): 193–206; Eric Van Dijk and Daan Van Knippenberg. "Buying and selling exchange goods: Loss aversion and the endowment effect." *Journal of Economic Psychology* 17, no. 4 (1996): 517–524.

6. Michael I. Norton, Daniel Mochon, and Dan Ariely. "The IKEA effect: When labor leads to love." *Journal of Consumer Psychology* 22, no. 3 (2012): 453–460; Marko Sarstedt, Doreen Neubert, and Kati Barth. "The IKEA effect. A conceptual replication." *Journal of Marketing Behavior* 2, no. 4 (2017): 307–312.

7. Jon Kabat-Zinn and Thich Nhat Hanh. *Full Catastrophe Living: Using the Wisdom of Your Body and Mind to Face Stress, Pain, and Illness.* New York: Bantam, 2009; Richard Shankman. *The Art and Skill of Buddhist Meditation: Mindfulness, Concentration, and Insight.* Oakland, CA: New Harbinger Publications, 2015.

Chapter 3

1. Jerry M. Burger. "Motivational biases in the attribution of responsibility for an accident: A meta-analysis of the defensive-attribution hypothesis." *Psychological Bulletin* 90, no. 3 (1981): 496–512; Incheol Choi and Richard E. Nisbett. "Situational salience and cultural differences in the correspondence bias and actor-observer bias." *Personality and Social Psychology Bulletin* 24, no. 9 (1998): 949–960; Bertram Gawronski. "Theory-based bias correction in dispositional inference: The fundamental attribution error is dead, long live the correspondence bias." *European Review of Social Psychology* 15, no. 1 (2004): 183–217; Daniel T. Gilbert and Patrick S. Malone. "The correspondence bias." *Psychological Bulletin* 117, no. 1 (1995): 21–38; Edward E. Jones and Victor A. Harris. "The attribution of attitudes." *Journal of Experimental Social Psychology* 3, no. 1 (1967): 1–24; Bertram F. Malle. "The actor-observer asymmetry in attribution: A (surprising) meta-analysis." *Psychological Bulletin* 132, no. 6 (2006): 895–919; Douglas S. Krull, Michelle Hui-Min Loy, Jennifer Lin, Ching-Fu Wang, Suhong Chen, and Xudong Zhao. "The fundamental fundamental attribution error: Correspondence bias in individualist and collectivist cultures." *Personality and Social Psychology Bulletin* 25, no. 10 (1999): 1208–1219; Lee Ross. "The intuitive psychologist and his shortcomings: Distortions in the attribution process." *Advances in Experimental Social Psychology*, vol. 10 (1977): 173–220.

2. Scott T. Allison and David M. Messick. "The group attribution error." *Journal of Experimental Social Psychology* 21, no. 6 (1985): 563–579; Olivier Corneille, Vincent Y. Yzerbyt, Anouk Rogier, and Geneviève Buidin. "Threat and the group attribution error: When threat elicits judgments of extremity and homogeneity." *Personality and Social Psychology Bulletin* 27, no. 4 (2001): 437–446; Ruth Hamill, Timothy D. Wilson, and Richard E. Nisbett. "Insensitivity to sample bias: Generalizing from atypical cases." *Journal of Personality and Social Psychology* 39, no. 4 (1980): 578–589; Diane M. Mackie and Scott T. Allison. "Group attribution errors and the illusion of group attitude change." *Journal of Experimental Social Psychology* 23, no. 6 (1987): 460–480.

3. Miles Hewstone. "The 'ultimate attribution error'? A review of the literature on intergroup causal attribution." *European Journal of Social Psychology* 20, no. 4 (1990): 311–335; Thomas F. Pettigrew. "The ultimate attribution error: Extending Allport's cognitive analysis of prejudice." *Personality and Social Psychology Bulletin* 5, no. 4 (1979): 461–476.

4. Frank Dobbin and Alexandra Kalev. "Why diversity programs fail And what works better." *Harvard Business Review* 94, no. 7–8 (2016): 52–60; Shari Caudron. "Training can damage diversity efforts." *Personnel Journal* 72, no. 4 (1993): 50–62; Benjamin Bowling. "Pulled over: How police stops define race and citizenship." *Policing and Society* (2018): 1–4; Patricia G. Devine, Patrick S. Forscher, Anthony J. Austin, and William T. L. Cox. "Long-term reduction in implicit race bias: A prejudice habit-breaking intervention." *Journal of Experimental Social Psychology* 48, no. 6 (2012): 1267–1278; John F. Dovidio, Kerry Kawakami, and Samuel L. Gaertner. "Reducing contemporary prejudice: Combating explicit and implicit bias at the individual and intergroup level." *Reducing Prejudice and Discrimination* (2000): 137–163; Anthony Greenwald and Linda Hamilton Krieger. "Implicit bias: Scientific foundations." *California Law Review* 94, no. 4 (2006): 945–967; Irene Frieze, Irene Hanson, Josephine E. Olson, and Deborah Cain Good. "Perceived and actual discrimination in the salaries of male and female managers." *Journal of Applied Social Psychology* 20, no. 1 (1990): 46–67; Hellen Hemphill and Ray Haines. *Discrimination, Harassment, and the Failure of Diversity Training: What to Do Now.* Westport, CT: Greenwood Publishing Group, 1997; Jasmin Joecks, Kerstin Pull, and Karin Vetter. "Gender diversity in the boardroom and firm performance: What exactly constitutes a 'critical mass?'" *Journal of Business Ethics* 118, no. 1 (2013): 61–72; John T. Jost, Laurie A. Rudman, Irene V. Blair, Dana R. Carney, Nilanjana Dasgupta, Jack Glaser, and Curtis D. Hardin. "The existence of implicit bias is beyond reasonable doubt: A refutation of ideological and methodological objections and executive summary of ten studies that no manager should ignore." *Research in Organizational Behavior* 29 (2009): 39–69; Karen S. Lyness and Donna E. Thompson. "Climbing the corporate ladder: Do female and male executives follow the same route?" *Journal of Applied Psychology* 85,

no. 1 (2000): 86–101; Ann M. Morrison and Mary Ann Von Glinow. "Women and minorities in management." *American Psychological Association* 45, no. 2: 1990; Marcus Noland, Tyler Moran, and Barbara Kotschwar. "Is gender diversity profitable? Evidence from a global survey." Peterson Institute for International Economics Working Paper No. 16–3 (2016): 1–35; Howard J. Ross, *Reinventing Diversity: Transforming Organizational Community to Strengthen People, Purpose, and Performance.* Lanham, MD: Rowman & Littlefield, 2011; Howard J. Ross and Jon Robert Tartaglione. *Our Search for Belonging: How Our Need to Connect Is Tearing Us Apart.* Oakland, CA: Berrett-Koehler Publishers, 2018; Linda K. Stroh, Jeanne M. Brett, and Anne H. Reilly. "All the right stuff: A comparison of female and male managers' career progression." *Journal of Applied Psychology* 77, no. 3 (1992): 251–260; David A. Thomas. "The impact of race on managers' experiences of developmental relationships (mentoring and sponsorship): An intra-organizational study." *Journal of Organizational Behavior* 11, no. 6 (1990): 479–492.

5. J. D. Trout. *The Empathy Gap: Building Bridges to the Good Life and the Good Society.* New York: Penguin, 2009; Karl-Andrew Woltin, Vincent Y. Yzerbyt, and Olivier Corneille. "On reducing an empathy gap: The impact of self-construal and order of judgment." *British Journal of Social Psychology* 50, no. 3 (2011): 553–562; Loran F. Nordgren, Kasia Banas, and Geoff MacDonald. "Empathy gaps for social pain: Why people underestimate the pain of social suffering." *Journal of Personality and Social Psychology* 100, no. 1 (2011): 120–128.

6. Robyn M. Dawes. "False consensus effect." *Insights in Decision Making: A Tribute to Hillel J. Einhorn* (1990): 179–199; Gary Marks and Norman Miller. "Ten years of research on the false-consensus effect: An empirical and theoretical review." *Psychological Bulletin* 102, no. 1 (1987): 72–90; Lee Ross, David Greene, and Pamela House. "The 'false consensus effect': An egocentric bias in social perception and attribution processes." *Journal of Experimental Social Psychology* 13, no. 3 (1977): 279-301.

7. Herman Aguinis, Harry Joo, and Ryan K. Gottfredson. "What monetary rewards can and cannot do: How to show employees the money." *Business*

Horizons 56, no. 2 (2013): 241–249; Martin Dewhurst, Matthew Guthridge, and Elizabeth Mohr. "Motivating people: Getting beyond money." *McKinsey Quarterly* 1, no. 4 (2009): 12–15; John Gibbons. *Employee Engagement*. New York: Pitman, 2006; Fraya Wagner-Marsh and James Conley. "The fourth wave: The spiritually-based firm." *Journal of Organizational Change Management* 12, no. 4 (1999): 292–302; Brent D. Rosso, Kathryn H. Dekas, and Amy Wrzesniewski. "On the meaning of work: A theoretical integration and review." *Research in Organizational Behavior* 30 (2010): 91–127; Michael F. Steger, Bryan J. Dik, and Ryan D. Duffy. "Measuring meaningful work: The work and meaning inventory (WAMI)." *Journal of Career Assessment* 20, no. 3 (2012): 322–337; Gleb Tsipursky. "Meaning and purpose in a non-Western modernity." *International Journal of Existential Psychology and Psychotherapy* 6, no. 1 (2016): 1–13; Gleb Tsipursky. *Find Your Purpose Using Science*. Columbus, OH: Intentional Insights, 2015.

8. Cedric Herring. "Does diversity pay? Race, gender, and the business case for diversity." *American Sociological Review* 74, no. 2 (2009): 208–224.

9. Sander Hoogendoorn, Hessel Oosterbeek, and Mirjam Van Praag. "The impact of gender diversity on the performance of business teams: Evidence from a field experiment." *Management Science* 59, no. 7 (2013): 1514–1528.

Chapter 4

1. Tracy Rucinski. "HCR ManorCare files for bankruptcy with $7.1 billion in debt." *Reuters*, Mar. 5, 2018, *www.reuters.com*

2. Mark Murphy. "Leadership IQ study: Mismanagement, inaction among the real reasons why CEOs get fired." Oct. 26, 2018, *www.prweb.com*

3. H. G. Parsa, John T. Self, David Njite, and Tiffany King. "Why restaurants fail." *Cornell Hotel and Restaurant Administration Quarterly* 46, no. 3 (2005): 304–322.

4. Richard S. Tedlow. *Denial: Why Business Leaders Fail to Look Facts in the*

Face and What to Do About It. New York: Penguin, 2010.

5. Clayton M. Christensen, Richard Alton, Curtis Rising, and Andrew Waldeck. "The big idea: The new M&A playbook." *Harvard Business Review* 89, no. 3 (2011): 48–57.

6. James Friedrich. "Primary error detection and minimization (PEDMIN) strategies in social cognition: A reinterpretation of confirmation bias phenomena." *Psychological Review* 100, no. 2 (1993): 298–319; Ivan Hernandez and Jesse Lee Preston. "Disfluency disrupts the confirmation bias." *Journal of Experimental Social Psychology* 49, no. 1 (2013): 178–182; Martin Jones and Robert Sugden. "Positive confirmation bias in the acquisition of information." *Theory and Decision* 50, no. 1 (2001): 59–99; Joshua Klayman. "Varieties of confirmation bias." *Psychology of Learning and Motivation* 32 (1995): 385–418; Jeffrey J. McMillan and Richard A. White. "Auditors' belief revisions and evidence search: The effect of hypothesis frame, confirmation bias, and professional skepticism." *Accounting Review* (1993): 443–465; Rosemarie Mendel, Eva Traut-Mattausch, Eva Jonas, Stefan Leucht, John M. Kane, Katja Maino, Werner Kissling, and Johannes Hamann. "Confirmation bias: Why psychiatrists stick to wrong preliminary diagnoses." *Psychological Medicine* 41, no. 12 (2011): 2651–2659; Geoffrey D. Munro and Jessica A. Stansbury. "The dark side of self-affirmation: Confirmation bias and illusory correlation in response to threatening information." *Personality and Social Psychology Bulletin* 35, no. 9 (2009): 1143–1153; Gleb Tsipursky. "How can facts trump ideology?" *The Human Prospect* 6, no. 3 (2017): 4–10.

7. Soma Biswas. "HCR ManorCare Files for Bankruptcy." *Wall Street Journal*, Mar. 5, 2018, *www.wsj.com*

8. Jack Ewing. "Ex-Volkswagen C.E.O. charged with fraud over diesel emissions." *New York Times*, May 3, 2018, *www.nytimes.com*

9. J. St. B.T. Evans, S. E. Newstead, J. L. Allen, and P. Pollard. "Debiasing by instruction: The case of belief bias." *European Journal of Cognitive Psychology* 6, no. 3 (1994): 263–285; Donna Torrens. "Individual differences and the belief bias effect: Mental models, logical necessity, and abstract reasoning." *Thinking & Reasoning* 5, no. 1 (1999): 1–28;

Walter C. Sá, Richard F. West, and Keith E. Stanovich. "The domain specificity and generality of belief bias: Searching for a generalizable critical thinking skill." *Journal of Educational Psychology* 91, no. 3 (1999): 497–510.

10. Dan Galai and Orly Sade. "The 'ostrich effect' and the relationship between the liquidity and the yields of financial assets." *The Journal of Business* 79, no. 5 (2006): 2741–2759; Niklas Karlsson, George Loewenstein, and Duane Seppi. "The ostrich effect: Selective attention to information." *Journal of Risk and Uncertainty* 38, no. 2 (2009): 95–115.

11. Haim Omer and Nahman Alon. "The continuity principle: A unified approach to disaster and trauma." *American Journal of Community Psychology* 22, no. 2 (1994): 273–287; Pamela V. Valentine and Thomas Edward Smith. "Finding something to do: The disaster continuity care model." *Brief Treatment and Crisis Intervention* 2, no. 2 (2002): 183–196.

12. John Eisenhammer, Colin Brown, and John Willcock, "Bank of England offloads blame for Barings collapse." *The Independent*, July 19, 1995, *www.independent.co.uk*

13. Ryan S. Bisel, Amber S. Messersmith, and Katherine M. Kelley. "Supervisor-subordinate communication: Hierarchical mum effect meets organizational learning." *The Journal of Business Communication (1973)* 49, no. 2 (2012): 128–147; Wing S. Chow and Lai Sheung Chan. "Social network, social trust and shared goals in organizational knowledge sharing." *Information & Management* 45, no. 7 (2008): 458–465; Jayson L. Dibble and Timothy R. Levine. "Breaking good and bad news: Direction of the MUM effect and senders' cognitive representations of news valence." *Communication Research* 37, no. 5 (2010): 703–722; Sidney Rosen and Abraham Tesser. "On reluctance to communicate undesirable information: The MUM effect." *Sociometry* (1970): 253–263; Eliezer Yariv. "'MUM effect'": Principals' reluctance to submit negative feedback." *Journal of Managerial Psychology* 21, no. 6 (2006): 533–546.

14. Constantine W. Sedikides, Keith Campbell, Glenn D. Reeder, and Andrew J. Elliot. "The self-serving bias in relational context." *Journal of Personality and Social Psychology* 74, no. 2 (1998): 378–386.

15. Lisa K. Fazio, Nadia M. Brashier, B. Keith Payne, and Elizabeth J. Marsh. "Knowledge does not protect against illusory truth." *Journal of Experimental Psychology: General* 144, no. 5 (2015): 993–1002.

16. Xiang Fang, Surendra Singh, and Rohini Ahluwalia. "An examination of different explanations for the mere-exposure effect." *Journal of Consumer Research* 34, no. 11 (2007): 97–103.

17. Scot Burton, Laurel Aynne Cook, Elizabeth Howlett, and Christopher L. Newman. "Broken halos and shattered horns: Overcoming the biasing effects of prior expectations through objective information disclosure." *Journal of the Academy of Marketing Science* 43, no. 2 (2015): 240–256; Michelle C. Bligh, Jeffrey C. Kohles, Craig L. Pearce, Joseph E. Justin, and John F. Stovall. "When the romance is over: Follower perspectives of aversive leadership." *Applied Psychology* 56, no. 4 (2007): 528–557; Lance Leuthesser, Chiranjeev S. Kohli, and Katrin R. Harich. "Brand equity: The halo effect measure." *European Journal of Marketing* 29, no. 4 (1995): 57–66; Richard E. Nisbett and Timothy D. Wilson. "The halo effect: Evidence for unconscious alteration of judgments." *Journal of Personality and Social Psychology* 35, no. 4 (1977): 250–256; W. Timothy Coombs and Sherry J. Holladay. "Unpacking the halo effect: Reputation and crisis management." *Journal of Communication Management* 10, no. 2 (2006): 123–137.

18. Praveen Aggarwal Stephen B. Castleberry, Rick Ridnour, and C. David Shepherd. "Salesperson empathy and listening: Impact on relationship outcomes." *Journal of Marketing Theory and Practice* 13, no. 3 (2005): 16–31; Peter Edelman and Daan van Knippenberg. "Emotional intelligence, management of subordinate's emotions, and leadership effectiveness." *Leadership & Organization Development Journal* 39, no. 5 (2018): 592–607; Tomas R. Giberson, Christian J. Resick, Marcus W. Dickson, Jacqueline K. Mitchelson, Kenneth R. Randall, and Malissa A. Clark. "Leadership and organizational culture: Linking CEO characteristics to cultural values." *Journal of Business and Psychology* 24, no. 2 (2009): 123–137; Bryce G. Hoffman. *American Icon: Alan Mulally and the*

Fight to Save Ford Motor Company. New York: Three Rivers Press, 2012; Rob H. Kamery. "Motivation techniques for positive reinforcement: A review." In *Allied Academies International Conference. Academy of Legal, Ethical and Regulatory Issues. Proceedings*, vol. 8, no. 2 (2004): 91–96; John D. Mayer and Glenn Geher. "Emotional intelligence and the identification of emotion." *Intelligence* 22, no. 2 (1996): 89–113; Robin T. Peterson and Yam Limbu. "The convergence of mirroring and empathy: Communications training in business-to-business personal selling persuasion efforts." *Journal of Business-to-Business Marketing* 16, no. 3 (2009): 193–219; Al Pittampalli. *Persuadable: How Great Leaders Change Their Minds to Change the World*. New York: Harper Business, 2016.

Chapter 5

1. Sydney Finkelstein. *Why Smart Executives Fail: And What You Can Learn from Their Mistakes*. New York: Penguin, 2004; Jayashree Mahajan. "The overconfidence effect in marketing management predictions." *JMR, Journal of Marketing Research* 29, no. 3 (1992): 329–342; Ulrike Malmendier and Geoffrey Tate. "CEO overconfidence and corporate investment." *The Journal of Finance* 60, no. 6 (2005): 2661–2700; Richard F. West and Keith E. Stanovich. "The domain specificity and generality of overconfidence: Individual differences in performance estimation bias." *Psychonomic Bulletin & Review* 4, no. 3 (1997): 387–392; Mark D. Alicke and Olesya Govorun. "The better-than-average effect." *The Self in Social Judgment* 1 (2005): 85–106.

2. R. Bénabou. "Groupthink: Collective delusions in organizations and markets." *Review of Economic Studies,* 80(2) (2012): 429–462.

3. Lisa Everson and Kim Bainbridge. "How Jeni's Splendid Ice Creams handled a listeria crisis." *NBC News*, Feb. 26, 2018, *www.nbcnews.com*

4. Deloitte. "The state of the deal: M&A trends 2018." (2018): 1–24. *www2.deloitte.com*

5. KPMG, "Unlocking shareholder value: The keys to success." (1999): 1–21, *http://people.stern.nyu.edu*

6. Ola Svenson. "Are we all less risky and more skillful than our fellow drivers?" *Acta Psychologica* 47, no. 2 (1981): 143–148.

7. Ezra W. Zuckerman and John T. Jost. "What makes you think you're so popular? Self-evaluation maintenance and the subjective side of the 'friendship paradox.'" *Social Psychology Quarterly* (2001): 207–223.

8. Myles Udland. "Fidelity reviewed which investors did best and what they found was hilarious." *Business Insider*, Sept. 4, 2014, *www.businessinsider.com*

9. David Dunning. "The Dunning–Kruger effect: On being ignorant of one's own ignorance." *Advances in Experimental Social Psychology*, vol. 44 (2011): 247–296; Justin Kruger and David Dunning. "Unskilled and unaware of it: How difficulties in recognizing one's own incompetence lead to inflated self-assessments." *Journal of Personality and Social Psychology* 77, no. 6 (1999): 1121–1134; Oliver Sheldon, David Dunning, and Daniel R. Ames. "Emotionally unskilled, unaware, and uninterested in learning more: Reactions to feedback about deficits in emotional intelligence." *Journal of Applied Psychology* 99, no. 1 (2014): 125–137.

10. Chunka Mui and Paul Carroll. *Billion Dollar Lessons*. New York: Portfolio, 2008.

11. Hal R. Arkes, David Faust, Thomas J. Guilmette, and Kathleen Hart. "Eliminating the hindsight bias." *Journal of Applied Psychology* 73, no. 2 (1988): 305–307; Hal R. Arkes, Robert L. Wortmann, Paul D. Saville, and Allan R. Harkness. "Hindsight bias among physicians weighing the likelihood of diagnoses." *Journal of Applied Psychology* 66, no. 2 (1981): 252–254.

12. Jeon Wook Son and Eddy M. Rojas. "Impact of optimism bias regarding organizational dynamics on project planning and control." *Journal of Construction Engineering and Management* 137, no. 2 (2010): 147–157; Bent Flyvbjerg. "Curbing optimism bias and strategic misrepresentation in planning: Reference class forecasting in practice." *European Planning Studies* 16, no. 1 (2008): 3–21.

13. Dariusz Dolinski, Wojciech Gromski, and Ewa Zawisza. "Unrealistic pessimism." *The Journal of Social Psychology* 127, no. 5 (1987): 511–516.

14. Roger Buehler, Dale Griffin, and Michael Ross. "Exploring the 'planning fallacy': Why people underestimate their task completion times." *Journal of Personality and Social Psychology* 67, no. 3 (1994): 366–81; Markus K. Brunnermeier, Filippos Papakonstantinou, and Jonathan A. Parker. "An economic model of the planning fallacy." No. 14228. *National Bureau of Economic Research*, 2008; Roger Buehler, Dale Griffin, and Johanna Peetz. "The planning fallacy: Cognitive, motivational, and social origins." *Advances in Experimental Social Psychology* 43 (2010): 1–62; Justin Kruger, and Matt Evans. "If you don't want to be late, enumerate: Unpacking reduces the planning fallacy." *Journal of Experimental Social Psychology* 40, no. 5 (2004): 586–598.

15. Thomas Gilovich, Kenneth Savitsky, and Victoria Husted Medvec. "The illusion of transparency: Biased assessments of others' ability to read one's emotional states." *Journal of Personality and Social Psychology* 75, no. 2 (1998): 332–346; Leaf Van Boven, Thomas Gilovich, and Victoria Husted Medvec. "The illusion of transparency in negotiations." *Negotiation Journal* 19, no. 2 (2003): 117–131.

16. James Surowiecki. *The Wisdom of Crowds*. Anchor, 2005; Jack Zenger and Joseph Folkman. "Ten fatal flaws that derail leaders." *Harvard Business Review* 87, no. 6 (2009): 18–22.

Chapter 6

1. N. Amir, J. Elias, H. Klumpp, and A. Przeworski. "Attentional bias to threat in social phobia: Facilitated processing of threat or difficulty disengaging attention from threat?" *Behaviour Research and Therapy* 41, no. 11 (2003): 1325–1335; Yair Bar-Haim, Dominique Lamy, Lee Pergamin, Marian J. Bakermans-Kranenburg, and Marinus H. Van Ijzendoorn. "Threat-related attentional bias in anxious and nonanxious individuals: A meta-analytic study." *Psychological Bulletin* 133, no. 1 (2007): 1–24; Elaine Fox, Riccardo Russo, and Kevin Dutton.

"Attentional bias for threat: Evidence for delayed disengagement from emotional faces." *Cognition & Emotion* 16, no. 3 (2002): 355–379.

2. Jongwoon Choi, Gary W. Hecht, and William B. Tayler. "Strategy selection, surrogation, and strategic performance measurement systems." *Journal of Accounting Research* 51, no. 1 (2013): 105–133.

3. Jess Benhabib, Alberto Bisin, and Andrew Schotter. "Present-bias, quasi-hyperbolic discounting, and fixed costs." *Games and Economic Behavior* 69, no. 2 (2010): 205–223; David Laibson. "Golden eggs and hyperbolic discounting." *The Quarterly Journal of Economics* 112, no. 2 (1997): 443–478.

4. Jonathan Baron and Ilana Ritov. "Reference points and omission bias." *Organizational Behavior and Human Decision Processes* 59, no. 3 (1994): 475–498; Johanna H. Kordes-de Vaal. "Intention and the omission bias: Omissions perceived as nondecisions." *Acta Psychological* 93, no. 1–3 (1996): 161–172.

5. "Circuit City CEO resigns amid troubles." *The Mercury News*, Sept. 22, 2008, *www.mercurynews.com*

6. Glenn E. Littlepage and Julie R. Poole. "Time allocation in decision making groups." *Journal of Social Behavior and Personality* 8, no. 4 (1993): 663–672; Michael J. Oyster. "Performance Doesn't Tell the Whole Story." *Success in a Low-Return World*. Basingstoke, UK: Palgrave Macmillan, Cham, 2018, 77–86.

7. Jonathan Baron and John C. Hershey. "Outcome bias in decision evaluation." *Journal of Personality and Social Psychology* 54, no. 4 (1988): 569–579; Philip J. Mazzocco, Mark D. Alicke, and Teresa L. Davis. "On the robustness of outcome bias: No constraint by prior culpability." *Basic and Applied Social Psychology* 26, no. 2–3 (2004): 131–146.

8. Eugene F. Fama and Kenneth French. "Mutual fund performance." *Journal of Finance* 63, no. 1 (2008): 389–416; Burton G. Malkiel. "Returns from investing in equity mutual funds 1971 to 1991." *The Journal of Finance* 50, no. 2 (1995): 549–572; Dirk Nitzsche, Keith Cuthbertson, and Niall O'Sullivan. "Mutual fund performance." SSRN (2006): 1–86. *https://ssrn.com*

9. Stephen J. Brown, William Goetzmann, Roger G. Ibbotson, and Stephen A. Ross. "Survivorship bias in performance studies." *The Review of Financial Studies* 5, no. 4 (1992): 553–580; Jennifer N. Carpenter and Anthony W. Lynch. "Survivorship bias and attrition effects in measures of performance persistence." *Journal of Financial Economics* 54, no. 3 (1999): 337–374.

10. Noel M. Tichy and Warren G. Bennis. *Judgment: How Winning Leaders Make Great Calls.* New York: Penguin, 2007.

11. Eugene Kim. "Jeff Bezos to employees: 'One day, Amazon will fail' but our job is to delay it as long as possible." *CNBC,* Nov. 27, 2018, *www. cnbc.com*

Index

versity and before that, a Fellow at the University of North Carolina at Chapel Hill. His dozens of peer-reviewed academic publications appear in journals such as *Behavior and Social Issues, Journal of Social and Political Psychology,* and *International Journal of Existential Psychology and Psychotherapy.*

His civic service include more than five years as the chair of the Board of Directors of Intentional Insights, an educational nonprofit advocating for research-based decision-making and truth-seeking in all life areas. He serves on the advisory boards of Canonical Debate Lab and Planet Purpose, and editorial board of the peer-reviewed journal *Behavior and Social Issues.*

Tsipursky earned his PhD in 2011 in the History of Behavioral Science at the University of North Carolina at Chapel Hill. He lives in Columbus, Ohio. In his free time, he enjoys tennis, hiking, and most importantly, spending abundant quality time with his wife to avoid disasters in his personal life. His website is *DisasterAvoidanceExperts.com,* and you can reach him via email at *Gleb@DisasterAvoidanceExperts.com.*

About the Author

Known as the Disaster Avoidance Expert, Dr. Gleb Tsipursky has more than twenty years of experience dramatically empowering leaders and organizations to avoid business disasters. He authored several books, most notably the bestseller *The Truth-Seeker's Handbook: A Science-Based Guide*, which tells readers how to avoid professional and other disasters by seeing reality clearly. Tsipursky's cutting-edge thought leadership has been featured in more than 400 published articles and more than 350 interviews with popular venues such as *Fast Company, CBS News, Time, Scientific American, Psychology Today, The Conversation, Business Insider, Government Executive*, CNBC, NPR, and *Inc. Magazine*.

Tsipursky's expertise comes from more than twenty years of consulting and coaching for businesses and nonprofits. He serves as the CEO of the boutique consulting, coaching, and training firm Disaster Avoidance Experts, which maximizes the bottom line for its clients by using a proprietary methodology based on cutting-edge research to address potential threats, maximize unexpected opportunities, and resolve persistent personnel problems. Tsipursky has personally worked with more than one hundred clients, some of which include Aflac, Fifth Third Bank, Honda, IBM, and Nationwide.

A highly in-demand international speaker, Tsipursky has more than two decades of professional speaking experience across North America, Europe, and Australia. He gets top marks from audiences for his highly facilitative, interactive, and humor-filled speaking style, as well as for thoroughly customizing speeches for diverse audiences.

Tsipursky has a strong research and teaching background in behavioral economics and neuroscience with more than fifteen years in academia, including seven years as a professor at the Ohio State Uni-